Rolling Shelter

Vehicles We Have Called Home

Book and cover design by the author

All photographs taken by either Kelly or Rosana Hart, except the cover photo and the photo on page 4, which were taken by visiting friends, and the photo of the author in his animation studio on page 14 taken by Wayne McCall, originally published in *Rescued Buildings*, published by Capra Press in 1977 and reprinted here by permission of the publisher.

Paperback ISBN: 0-916289-37-0

Printed in the United States of America

First printing August, 2013

Hartworks, Inc.
P. O. Box 632
Crestone, CO 81131

Email: theoffice@hartworks.com

Website: www.hartworks.com

Table of Contents

Foreword

Would you like to roam around in a vehicle that was your home, staying in beautiful natural settings and in urban areas, all the while earning your living and having a low overhead? That's what my husband Kelly Hart and I have done many times. How we did it, especially how we fixed up our buses, RVs, and other vehicle homes, is what this book is about.

I fell in love with Kelly when he was living in the first bus you'll see in the book. It was such a romantic little scene… how much was I falling in love with the location? That must not have been all, since we are still together after many a vehicle and several stationary homes. Van dwelling, RV living, boondocking in RVs and even in a station wagon… we've done it and loved it.

Living in tiny spaces, we quickly learned how to get along, since it was often hard to get away from each other. We still laugh ruefully about a huge argument we had once, on the road in Mexico, about which way to go! But generally, we are best friends and our travel styles are similar. Well, Kelly likes to get going sooner and I like to stay put longer, but it works out.

Life in rolling shelters is an adventure, and frequently things went wrong just when my patience and stamina were at low points. But we learned after a while that we usually had good bad luck—that is, we had bad luck like anyone does at times, but often something good came of it. We couldn't believe how often diesel mechanics materialized out of nowhere when we were full-timing in a diesel bus.

This book is meant to provide you with both how-to information and inspiration. While not everyone is going to remodel a bus, as Kelly did twice, you may get ideas for your own projects by seeing what we've done. Whether it's for vacation or for full-timing, whatever your finances are, do consider having your own rolling shelter! — Rosana Hart

Our family donned Hawaiian garb to pose for this Christmas card photo one year while we were converting our Grayline Hawaii tour bus into a motor home.

Introduction

This book will illustrate and describe some of my involvement with rolling shelter over several decades. My wife and I have lived in two different buses, three vans, two small motor homes, two travel trailers combined into one house, and two cars. My intention is to inspire you and give you some ideas for how you might take advantage of vehicles to provide shelter in your life.

Choosing to live in a vehicle can be ecologically worthwhile. One of the prime concepts of green living is to recycle things, rather than to buy new things that may have a negative impact on the environment. Certainly turning a used vehicle into a home fits this general principle, perhaps giving new life or purpose to something that would otherwise take up space in a junk yard. It isn't even necessary for a vehicular home to be in the greatest mechanical shape, since it may just be parked somewhere most of the time. In fact, if it doesn't run it can be towed from one place to another.

Another principle of green living is to occupy only as much space as is necessary for the functions intended. You don't need a large space to have a good life, that is for sure.

Living compactly has many advantages as well. It limits the impulse to buy stuff, simply because you don't have room to store it. And it is important to organize the space that you do have. An organized house leads to a more organized mind…and this is a good thing.

Also, if you can manage to create a home without going into debt, you are way ahead of the game in terms of making life choices that will lead to happiness. Mortgages ("death pledges" in French) can take an enormous toll on creativity and well being. We have done our best to avoid them.

Another tenet of sustainable living is to conserve energy and water resources. Dwelling in a small space obviously helps with this, since it takes much less energy to keep it comfortable and well lit. And often the capacity for storing fresh water and waste water is limited, which leads to a consciousness of conservation.

One factor in choosing to make a home out of a vehicle that isn't so obvious is that you can avoid dealing with restrictive building codes for the most part. Building authorities recognize that what you do with a vehicle is not within their jurisdiction. They might have an opinion about where the vehicle can be parked, but otherwise how it is put together is none of their business. Local authorities are interested in whether a vehicle is road worthy or not, and such mechanical issues can be addressed in conventional ways.

One of the true joys of living in a vehicle is that it can potentially be moved to new and wonderful locations with relative ease. Over the years, we have spent much time in absolutely glorious places. If you like to travel, but prefer to have your own bed and your own kitchen, then living in a motor home of some sort cannot be beat. There are many possibilities for where to park, from campgrounds to rest stops to friends' land to U. S. Forest Service land. Bear in mind that private land may have zoning laws or other covenants and restrictions that might limit where you can park or live in a motor home or vehicle. It is best to be aware of this before being rudely told to move on.

As climate change has become a harsh reality, you may want to limit the amount of gasoline you use. But you don't have to drive the vehicle for it to be useful. And when you do drive you don't have to go very far, and you can often stay in one location for months or years at a time. Many vehicle dwellers find that their gas usage is quite minimal.

Our First Bus Home

The first true home that was entirely mine was based in a vehicle. My first wife was pregnant and we really wanted to have our own place for our new family to live in. Buying a house was out of the question financially, so it occurred to me that maybe we could buy an old bus and turn it into a home on wheels.

I was living near Berkeley, California, at the time. With a little research I discovered that the Gillig bus manufacturing plant was located not far away. When I called to ask about possible used buses they might have gotten as trade-ins, they responded that, yes, indeed they had a number of them out in their yard that they would be happy to sell.

Many school buses are not really great for converting to a home because of limited head room, often having a well corridor running down the middle. But I found one bus, a 1952 Southern Coach that had been used as a school bus but was actually manufactured as an army transport vehicle. It had full 6 1/2 foot standing room. And like many items made to military specs, this bus was quite solidly built, with high quality components.

The skin, inside and out, as well as all of the window frames, was entirely aluminum…virtually indestructible. The space between the skins was insulated. The Waukesha gas engine was placed on its side under the floor right in the middle of the bus. This allowed the entire 30 ft length of the coach to be open and usable for living space.

I could afford their price, so I was soon driving this bus to park it in the back of my folks' place in

Berkeley, where my sister and brother-in-law had recently built a lovely sailboat.

I built the interior without a detailed plan in mind, except that I knew I wanted a permanent double bed in the back; otherwise, I just put things where it seemed appropriate. I wanted the stove to be near the center to distribute the heat and there was a convenient vent in the roof nearby for the stove pipe. We wanted the kitchen table near the stove so we could sit and watch the fire and be warm on the coldest night. We wanted the sink near the table for efficient movement of dishes, and so the design just fell into place.

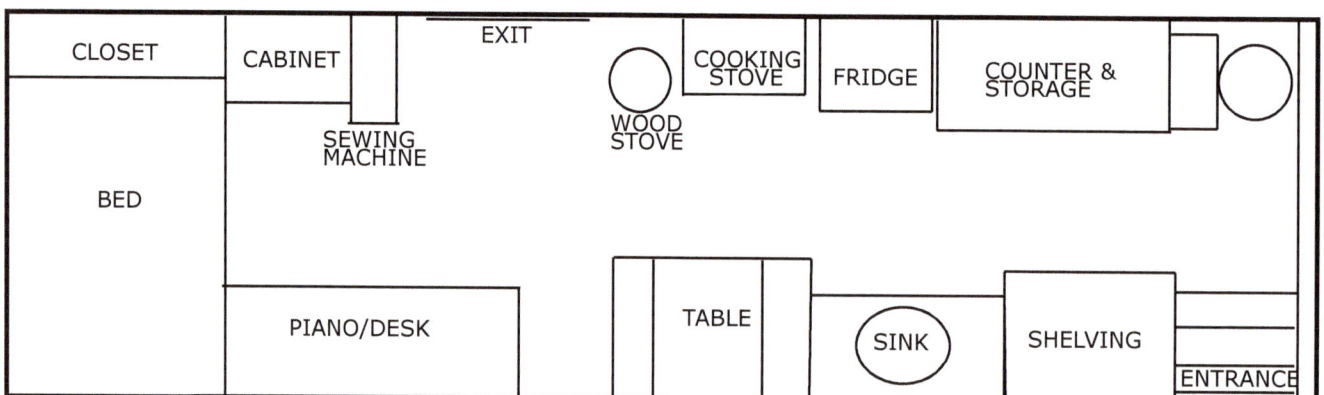

I found a really cute little antique pot-bellied wood stove that I was sure would put out plenty of heat for such a small space. Then I found a similar antique three-burner gas cook stove with a small oven, and I converted it to work with propane. To complete the set of appliances, I installed an old fashioned little apartment refrigerator. All of these lent considerable charm to this cozy dwelling.

What transformed the bus from a tunnel into a castle was the addition of six 2 1/2 ft. square dome skylights. I was working at the City of Berkeley's Art Center, where I made the acquaintance of an artist whose speciality was vacuum forming plastic art objects. I enlisted his help in fabricating these skylights that bulged in pairs between the framing members of the bus's roof. This brought in a tremendous amount of light, so much that I had to make rolling bamboo shades to block out the sun at times. In fact, in many climates putting in skylights would not be a good idea as it would tend to cook the interior. As it turned out, I parked the bus on the coast where the fog and cooler air made the skylights quite welcome.

My ultimate luxury was a full sized upright piano from which I stripped all of the cabinetry, leaving the essential strings, sounding board, key board and action. The keyboard was detachable and hinged so that it would hang down to conserve space. Another board fit into the place of the keys to serve as a work table.

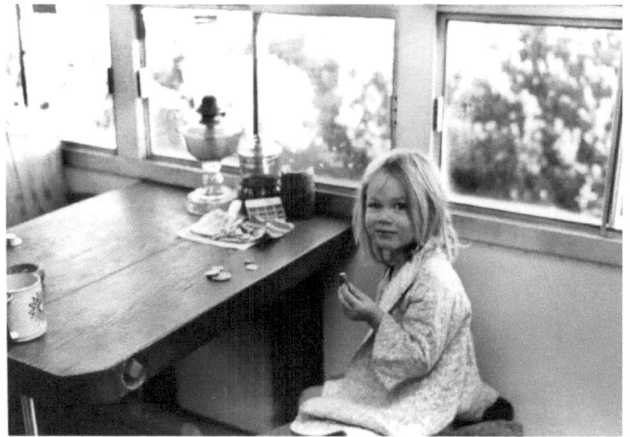

As with the piano/work table combination, there were several other multi-use facilities. The kitchen cutting board served as an ironing board (rarely used). The kitchen table was a three-inch slab of solid laminated fir, sturdy enough to knead bread or wedge clay. The steering wheel had a little typing table installed over it, and the driver's seat could be adjusted to the proper height.

We had some friends living in Jenner, at the mouth of the Russian River, and they were quite willing to allow us to park the bus on their land. They even let us use a lovely little bath house and toilet, along with water and electricity from their house. In exchange for this we helped out with fire wood collection and child care occasionally.

Above are pictured my then new and still current wife, Rosana, and my daughter Ajila.

I dug by hand a gravel-packed well (17 feet deep and 4 feet in diameter), and later built a small shower and toilet stall next to the bus to make life a bit more convenient. We even had a phone installed inside the bus.

I built a large semi-circular deck adjacent to the side of the bus with the emergency exit, providing open space for kids to play and for me to do my kung fu.

In 1972, after four years of living in the bus I wrote a short article for the original *Shelter* book by Lloyd Khan. Here are some of my thoughts at that time:

I find the bus at least as comfortable as any house I've lived in. The main reason why I got it in the first place is I was sick and tired of fixing up a rented

apartment or house to suit my needs, only to be forced by circumstances of ownership to look for another place.

This experiment in bus living has proved to be highly beneficial and instructive. In fact, I often have a feeling of claustrophobia when encased in a conventional dwelling, because the bus has 360 degree visibility plus all the light from the dome skylights.

The advantages of bus living are manyfold; to list a few of them:

Mobility…The fact that it is on wheels means that I am not permanently stuck in one locale…this gives me great freedom.

Durability…I was lucky to find a bus that was constructed almost entirely of aluminum so I don't have the problem of the thing rusting away, it is less vulnerable to fire…it's also practically impervious to earthquake damage…

Building codes…The bus is a vehicle, not a house, so it is properly under the jurisdiction of the motor vehicles department, not the housing authorities. When I was driving it I had it registered as a housecar and the registration fees were about $18 a year, but since it has been stationary I have not even paid this. You can't beat that for taxes!

Efficiency…Living in a compact space brings about efficiency in many spheres.

Heat…We have a small wood stove that keeps the bus cozy in any California weather…

Ventilation…With so many openable windows and doors, the bus can be thoroughly ventilated in any desired cross direction. The back opens up completely and there is an emergency exit in addition to the front door.

Movement...*The inside of the bus measures about 28'x8', or 224 sq. ft., so one need only move a few steps to arrive at any point within. It's amazing how such a simple fact can make life so much easier. Standing in the center of the bus (which is essentially the kitchen), we can easily reach anything with a few steps.*

Organization...*I feel that the real crux of successful life in a bus, or any other small space for that matter, lies in efficient organization and use of space. It would not be practical for some people to even attempt such a life because their habits and life styles do not blend with such a highly organized way of living. So if it pleases you to have a place for everything and everything in its place, then perhaps you could be happy in a bus.*

Furniture and fixtures...*Once I got the bus set up for living (this took about four months) and then chose the belongings I really needed and eliminated the rest, the temptation to shop for new furniture or pretties was severely curtailed. If I buy something and bring it home, I then have to find a place to put it. This has definitely curbed my spending urge.*

Housework...*There practically is none! It takes just a few minutes to sweep, the table can be cleared in a matter of seconds, and there just isn't very much area to keep clean.*

Of course there are some disadvantages to bus life that parallel life in any small space. Primary among these is that it gets pretty crowded when you get more than a few people spending very much time indoors, or that if you have small children, the confinement during inclement weather can drive you up the wall.

We happily lived in that bus for several years, until we decided to move on to other adventures outlined in the next chapters. The collage of photos at the right show various family members and moments of bus life during that time.

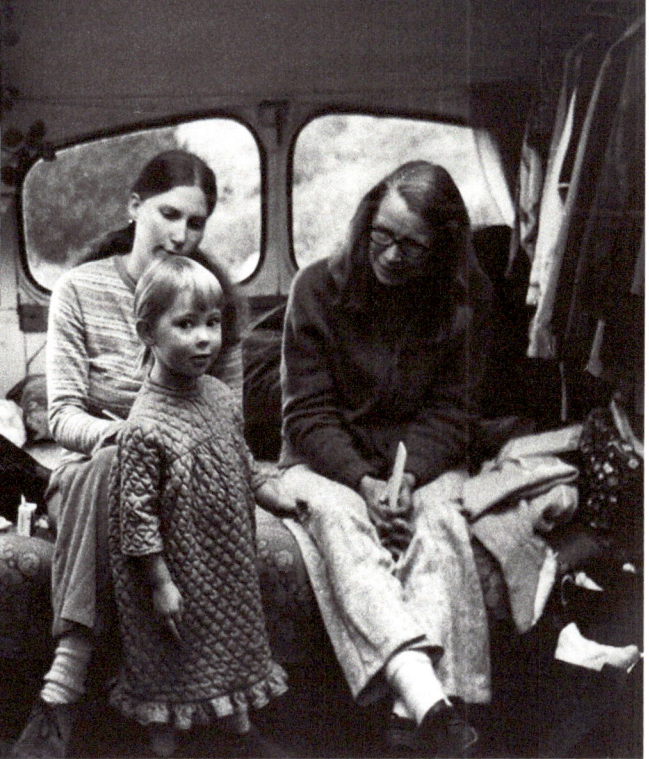

Extra Wheels

Around this time we added two more wheeled facilities to our fleet. First we bought a used step van that had been a laundry delivery vehicle. There was an extra bubble skylight left over from the bus project, so I mounted this in the middle of the roof to bring daylight into the back of the van. Otherwise the built-ins were minimal because I wanted this to be versatile as to how it got used. A simple bed platform provided sleeping space and a curtain could be pulled across to separate the cab from the back. With this arrangement, I could park it practically anywhere and have a very private place to spend time when I was away from my bus home.

I remember being awakened by the police banging on the door in the middle of the night once when I had parked the van on the waterfront in Oakland. They couldn't see inside, so I just kept quiet and they eventually left. Evidently it was illegal to sleep in vehicles in that location.

One of the ways that I made money in those days was to occasionally do carpentry and odd jobs for people, and this van was quite handy for transporting tools and supplies.

I also was developing a career as a film animator, since I had invented a process for making animated movies that I was patenting. There were times that I used the van as an animation studio, with equipment set up to do this. An animated sequence showing the evolution of mankind from a single cell to early man that I was commissioned to create for a feature film titled *The Naked Ape* was done in the back of that van. We also used the step van as guest space or getaway space when things got too hectic in the bus.

When I had the opportunity to purchase an old semi truck trailer that had been a portable military radar facility, I realized that this would make a much better film and animation studio. It was an ugly affair that was painted military green, so we just called it the "Green Box" and it became a useful part of my life for many years.

It was parked near the bus so my commute to work could not have been easier. The inside of the Green Box had dozens of built-in drawers and compartments, so it was great for organizing and storing equipment, as well as space for permanently setting up my animation equipment.

The big white billowing form in the photo shown below was our garden space. I created a greenhouse using an old surplus nylon parachute. Fencing kept the nosy deer away, and the parachute helped keep the incessant coastal winds at bay. The plants loved this protected environment; the light was diffused and it stayed slightly more humid in there. It wore out after a couple of seasons, but it was replaceable.

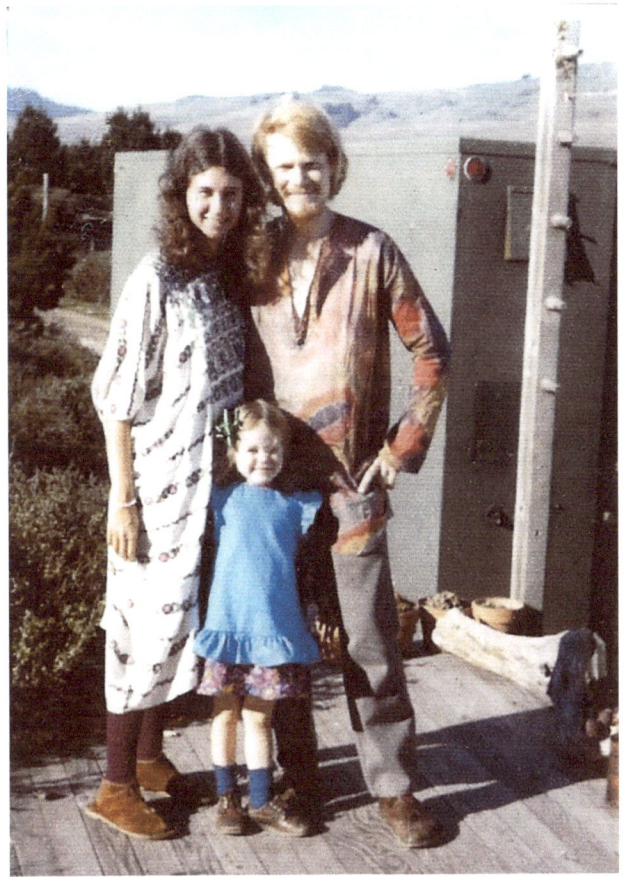

In the above photo you can see the lineup of step van, Green Box, and bus in the distance. To the right I am posing with Rosana, my second wife (we've now been married for over 40 years) and my daughter. Behind us is the Green Box.

Below you can see the collection of rolling stock after a rare coastal snow storm. The box with a pointed front is a car-top carrier that I made out of plywood to fit on the top our little VW Bug.

Above is a view of the inside of the Green Box with me doing animation. Below I am working in the parachute greenhouse.

Over to the right, our little family was on a road trip, visiting my parent's place in Idaho. The car-top carrier held most of our belongings. The back seat of the VW had been replaced with a platform, so that when we stopped for the night is was actually possible to take off the backs of the front seats and make a bed for sleeping. We didn't try this when traveling with my daughter, but Rosana and I did this several times…even traveling in Mexico!

After living in the bus for about seven years on the California coast, we pooled resources with two of my sisters and their families and bought some property further inland along the Russian River. We wanted to create a kind of family community, and the old summer camp that we bought was perfect for that.

So we moved the whole fleet to Forestville, California. The bus had remained stationary for over seven years and was not in drivable condition, so I hired a large tow truck to do the job of moving it.

You can read about our experience of living at Sunshine Camp in another book of my series about Green Home Building. Basically Rosana and I moved into a whole row of little cabins, and the bus was first used as office space for my sister's fledgling business, Folkware Patterns. Below you can see it parked on the left of the the entrance.

Then later it was moved again and became bedroom space for my other sister's growing family.

The Green Box was towed to a spot along the creek, up in the orchard, where it continued to serve as my animation studio.

Van Dwelling

Rosana and I decided we wanted to make a several month trip to Mexico and Guatemala. We no longer had the step van, having sold it to buy a communal pickup truck. So we started looking for just the right vehicle to live in as we meandered south. What we found was a Ford Econoline van that had already been converted to a camper van with a kind of pop top. We didn't really like the layout inside this, so I spent several weeks redesigning and rebuilding the interior.

This was a great little traveling home for us. We came up with a name for it, after we had traveled for some time in Mexico: Van Corazon. This was a play on Spanish/English meanings. "Van Corazon" in Spanish means "They go heart" and since our last name is "Hart," it also meant Hart's van. I even painted this on the bumper, following the Mexican tradition of putting names on their trucks. We also installed a little fringed curtain above the windshield.

Below is a diagram—not exactly to scale—of how the interior space was laid out. Ford Econoline vans of that vintage had their engines positioned between the driver and the passenger seats, under a cover that could be lifted to gain access to it. This meant you had to climb over the engine to get to the living area in the back. Otherwise there were a set of double doors to enter the space from the side.

I built a fairly conventional bed/table arrangement, where you have a choice of one or the other, but not both. The table lifted off some brackets attached to the back doors and would provide part of the bed platform. The benches provided the other part of the bed platform, and the rectangular cushions for the seats could be arranged as a mattress.

Here you can see Van Corazon fording a creek in Mexico. We traveled with the top collapsed to get better mileage. We had two 5 gallon propane tanks that I mounted on a bracket that hinged with the back door. On the other door is a spare tire. We used propane for a two-burner cook top and to run a small catalytic heater.

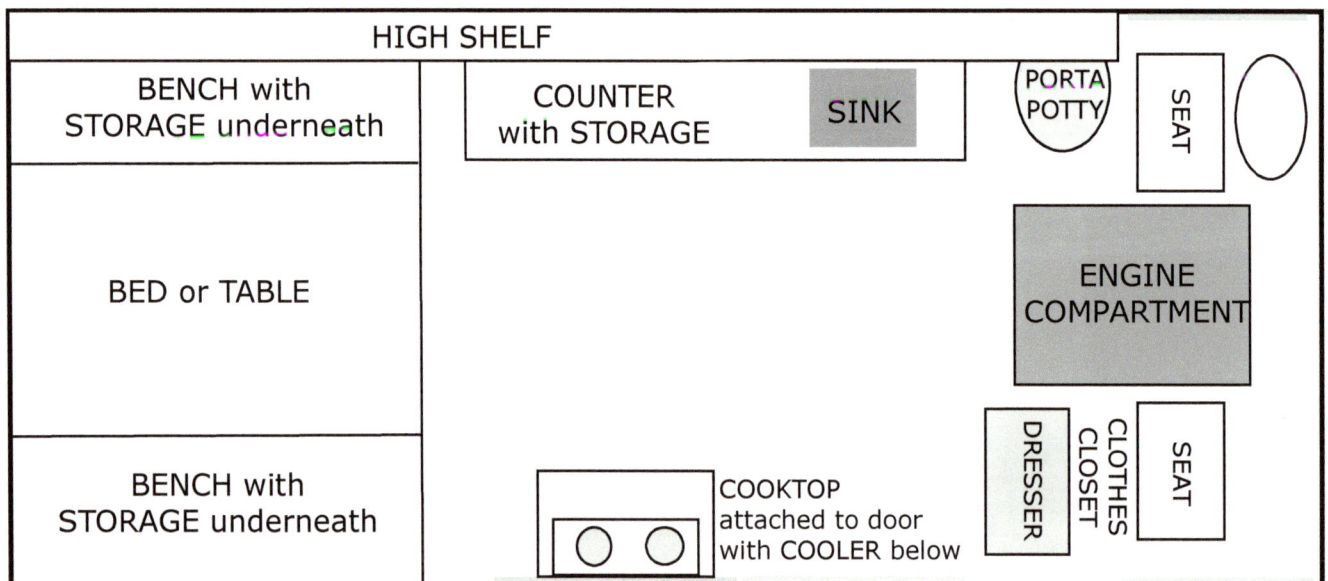

HIGH SHELF

BENCH with STORAGE underneath

COUNTER with STORAGE — SINK

PORTA POTTY — SEAT

BED or TABLE

ENGINE COMPARTMENT

BENCH with STORAGE underneath

COOKTOP attached to door with COOLER below

DRESSER — CLOTHES CLOSET — SEAT

A Porta Potty was located directly behind the driver's seat, which provided some privacy even while on the road. A kitchen counter with a tiny sink also had storage for food and cooking supplies beneath. There were several 5 gallon water containers that provided water for the little hand pump next to the sink. Another tank collected gray water from the sink. Up above the counter, all along that side of the van was a narrow shelf with a raised lip along the edge. This added a surprising amount of storage space.

Behind the passenger seat, wedged between the back of the seat and a small commercial dresser, we had a small space for a few clothes on hangers. The top of the dresser also had a raised lip around it, making a good place for quite a few books.

Attached to one of the side doors was a little propane cook top with two burners. This was convenient in that when the door was swung all the way open, we could cook outside, under a canopy that was attached to the outside of the van.

Directly below the cook top was an interesting cooling box, called a Coolatron, that ran on 12 volt DC. This device didn't keep things at a constant temperature like a refrigerator, but would keep the contents noticeably cooler than the ambient temperature.

We made this trip through Mexico and Guatemala in 1979 and had a wonderful time, bringing back many fond memories. We just meandered at will, parking in all kinds of places, sometimes just out in the open

country. Often we asked local people where they thought it would be safe to park overnight. (It was a more relaxed era and we were grateful for the kindness we encountered.)

Above, you can see how Van Corazon looked with the top popped up. To raise it, you had to get inside and push up on the two hinged sides. The metal top then conformed to the rounded shape of the sides. To let it back down you just reversed the movement. Very simple. I also built a rack on the roof, making it possible to carry long cargo when necessary.

There weren't that many designated RV camping facilities in Mexico then. When Mexicans went camping then, it was usually with a tent. We did find one nice campground (pictured above) in the state of Chiapas. Other gringos and their odd rigs surrounded us. We later encountered that same VW van down in Guatemala and renewed our acquaintance with the couple traveling in it.

Traveling in this way, we met many wonderful people. It seemed like wherever we parked, folks were curious about how our little "casita" was set up. People would say, "Oh, it has everything!"

Many times people standing on the side of the road would hail us to stop, and we wondered why until we realized that small vans like ours were commonly used as buses in rural areas. Sometimes we did stop and take people further along the road.

We met these women and children in a tiny village at the end of a long dirt road in Michoacan. They were very friendly and brought us some tortillas to eat. We parked under a palm tree for a couple of nights and had a great time. I pulled out my watercolors and did some sketching. I hoped to bring the bamboo lashed to the side of the van back home to the U.S., but agricultural inspection didn't like the idea.

Once we entered Guatemala the whole feeling of the countryside changed, becoming more mountainous and tropical. The native Mayans were just as friendly and curious as the Mexicans. One couple invited us into their house after we parked along the side of the road just a short distance across the border. They were very proud that they had running water piped into their house.

We visited Lake Atitlan and were enchanted by its beauty. Soon we became acquainted with a Chilean inventor who had some property overlooking the lake and he invited us to come and park on his land. We ended up staying there for a couple of weeks, during which time I painted the watercolor reproduced below.

Excursions to the local native markets were always a colorful and enriching experience. The Mayan weaving is lovely and we bought some to bring home. I was also taking photos and occasional movies, which I tried to do without being noticed because I knew that many of the people disliked it.

We had heard about a small village called Todos Santos, high in the mountains over an even higher pass. We decided to see if we could find it and took off in that direction. We managed to get up to the top of the pass that afternoon and parked among the huge boulders to spend the night. The image at the top of the next page shows our camping spot.

On the way down to Todos Santos it rained. We noticed quite a few Mayans walking along the side of the road, some of them swaying in a drunken fashion. One women motioned us to stop, so we did. She wanted us to help take her husband back home to the village because he was too drunk to walk. We helped them into the back of the van, and soon realized that we were in the midst of Semana Santa, a long holiday during which time the Mayans traditionally get drunk on their local alcohol concoction, which is very strong.

The woman held a scarf in her hands, obviously carefully cradling something. As we started on down the road, Rosana asked her what she was carrying, and she pulled back enough of the scarf to show us a little bird that she had caught and was taking home.

She also showed us some lovely woven purses she had made, and we asked if we could buy one. She said yes and it is still among our cherished possessions.

As we approached the village there was a particularly loud clap of thunder. The woman clutched her heart, exclaiming how frightened she was of the noise. Then she motioned us to stop next to a house on the outskirts of town, saying it was theirs. Her husband got out and went inside, but she wanted to stay in the van for a bit until the rain subsided.

Abruptly there was another loud crash, and she looked horrified. Eventually she got up her nerve to go into the house herself, saying that we were welcome to stay parked there if we wanted…or we could go down the street a ways and park by her uncle's house.

A few minutes later she came running back out of her house and knocked on our door. When we opened it she explained that the crash that we had heard was part of their house falling down! Evidently the heavy rain had undermined part of the foundation. Fortunately her husband was slumbering in the part of the house that had not collapsed.

Wow…what an introduction to Todos Santos! We decided to move down the street a bit to park for the night, fearing that some of the locals might associate our presence with the house collapsing.

We didn't get a whole lot of sleep that night, what with the excitement of the day and the ongoing holiday revelry in the street. I remember the marimbas droning on endlessly.

Altogether we spent about a month exploring Guatemala and two months in Mexico. By the time we were ready to return home, the van was so stuffed with things we had bought for gifts or for ourselves that we could hardly move in there.

Not long after we returned home to Sunshine Camp we realized that my two sisters' marriages were beginning to unravel. We all decided that the best thing to do was to sell the property. It took us about a year to do this, with Rosana and me holding down the fort by ourselves toward the end.

The two of us explored other places to live, and took Van Corazon on several outings to do so. Eventually we settled near Ashland, Oregon, and that story is revealed in the next chapter.

This vehicle was fairly economical to run and served us well for several trips, but we found the engine to be basically underpowered for what we asked of it, so we decided to sell it to a mechanic friend.

We later traveled in two other camping vehicles that I want to describe here. One was a VW Vanagon camper with a different kind of pop top arrangement. It was already set up as a simple camper and the space was moderately efficient, so we didn't change it much. The sink was right at the entrance and there was a little hinging table that could be used when the door was open. In the back was a conventional bed/table affair.

Our other travelling home was a Volvo station wagon. This was a very solid car that we kept for over a decade. I remember one long vacation trip that we made up through Canada when we camped almost exclusively in the Volvo. A permanent mattress was fitted in the space behind the front seats. We had curtains that would velcro into place for privacy. Some luggage and other items had to be put in the front when we slept at night. Minimal, but effective!

Juniper Ridge

After we sold Sunshine Camp, Rosana and I were ready to have our own place again, without the constraints that communal life can bring. We made several trips in Van Corazon, looking for possible locations where we could establish a new life. We wanted a place with rural beauty yet close to some urban amenities.

A friend had suggested that we take a look at Ashland, Oregon. We found it quite appealing with much of what we were looking for, but the local real estate was fairly expensive. We circled around the vicinity and discovered that a huge ranch south of Ashland was in the process of being divided into parcels for sale. We left word at the real estate office that we would be interested in any property that became available not too far from Ashland.

A few months later they contacted us saying that there were a number of parcels now for sale within about 10 to 20 miles of Ashland. They sent us a map of these. Most of the property was down in the valley on the other side of the Siskiyou summit, which meant that it was rather remote in terms of access to

the town of Ashland. But then we noticed one piece that was actually adjacent to the Mount Ashland Ski Road and only about a mile away from the freeway into town. This 70 acre parcel was high up along the ridge overlooking both the Klamath River basin on one side and the Rogue River basin on the other, so the views would be phenomenal.

We dashed right up from California to take a look and were bowled over by the magnificent beauty. It didn't take us very long to make on offer on this property, and soon we were owners of land that was comparable in beauty to any national park I have seen. We were ecstatic!

The photo below shows Van Corazon parked at the entrance to our new property. That's about as far as we could drive in due to the snow. We didn't even have to establish a new access road to the property, as this lane up to the ridge was already there.

This was 70 acres of bare land that had never been lived on before. The road had probably been established to do some logging many years before. At the top of the ridge there was an old well that we were told had never been used because it was unproductive.

Above is the view to the south from the top of the ridge. It would be a possible view from any house we might build. The tall peak on the left is Mount Shasta in Northern California. The valley below us was filled with fog, as was often the case, but we got a lot of sunshine up there.

Most of the land sloped abruptly down from this point, with some portions of sheer rock cliffs plunging down to protected glens of Big Leaf Maple and pine trees. At the top of the property, along the ridge, were mostly old gnarled Juniper trees, which is why we eventually decided to call the land Juniper Ridge.

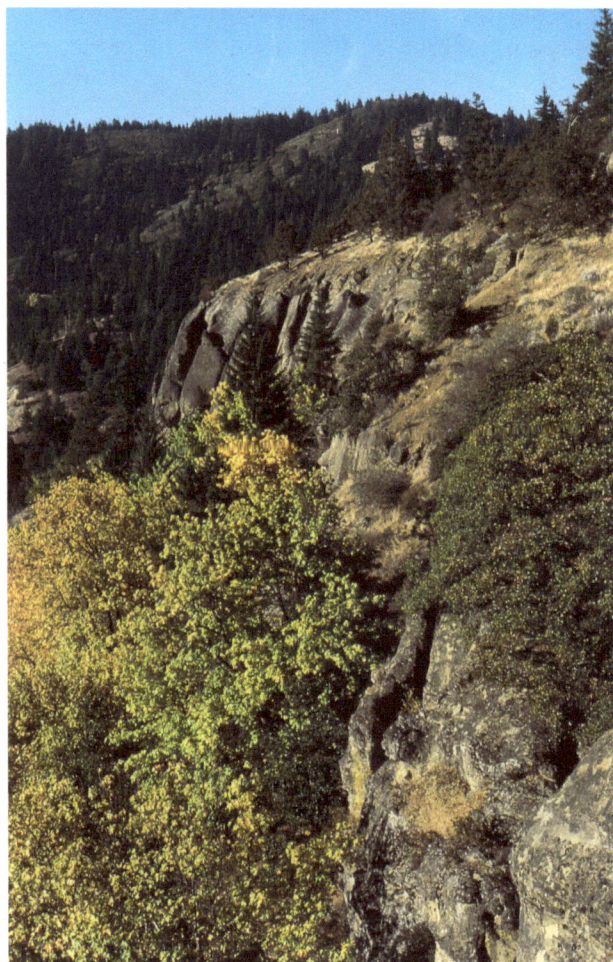

We spent many days just hiking around the property and dreaming about what we might do there. It had taken most of our money just to buy the land, so our dreaming was not too extravagant.

We were still living down in California and only came up to camp on the land when we could get away. But eventually we were ready to move to Oregon for good. We packed the Green Box with much of our stuff and hired a trucker to haul it up there.

Besides Van Corazon, we also had an old diesel Mercedes Benz sedan to drive to Oregon. Plus we had two dogs and a cat to transport. So we caravaned up to Juniper Ridge in the summer when the weather was good enough to camp there.

In the above photo you can see how we were set up when the Green Box arrived. I had cleared a spot up near the top of the ridge amongst some willow trees where I had the trucker nestle the Box into its new home. At this point all of our earthly possessions were assembled in it. We had included the old bus as part of the deal when we sold Sunshine Camp.

Almost as soon as we were established there we woke up one morning to the smell of smoke in the air. It didn't take us long to realize that there was a forest fire down in the valley below us, perhaps five miles away…and it was moving in our direction!

Soon we heard fire engines and then there were planes flying overhead, barely skimming the ridge on their way to dump loads of retardant on the fire. There wasn't much we could do but watch and hope that the wind changed direction. Perhaps the rock cliff would afford some measure of protection, but I wasn't willing to bet on it.

We met many of our neighbors for the first time when they drove up to our land to get a view of the fire, as it was the best vantage point to see the whole scope of it. It was thought that the fire was started by a spark from a train passing along the tracks below.

I think that the fire chief of the small volunteer fire department down in the valley was the first to notice the fire, as it started quite near his house.

After about twenty four hours, the wind abruptly changed direction and started blowing the fire the opposite way, back into the area that had already burned. What a relief! Not long after that the fire was declared contained, but it still smoldered for several days. We felt like we had somehow passed a trial by fire on our new land and were now blessed with opportunities to manifest our new life there.

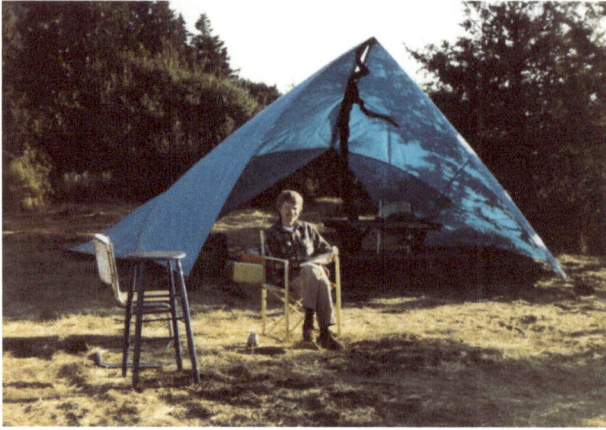

Besides Van Corazon and the stuffed Green Box, our only other shelter was this tent arrangement made with a couple of tarps.

We arranged for the power company to extend the electricity from about a half mile away to a spot close to where we intended to build.

We decided to look for a cheap trailer that we could buy to at least get a foothold on the property, even if it were only temporary. In scanning the local classified ads, we noticed one for a 40 foot long travel trailer that said "For Sale or Trade: Make Offer." This was in a city about 40 miles away, so we decided to go and take a look.

The trailer was in reasonably good shape, had real wood cabinetry inside, and looked like we could make do with it, at least for awhile. Almost as a lark, we offered our old Mercedez Benz diesel car in trade. We knew that we were going to have to get a differ-

ent car anyway, one that could deal better with with the snow and ice in the winter.

To our surprise the sellers said, yes, they would make that trade! Great. We still had to pay to have the trailer towed to our land, but that was a small price to pay for a house.

We got busy preparing a spot near the top of the ridge, where we would have wonderful views toward Mt. Shasta to the south, and we would get good passive solar heat into the trailer. The spot was already fairly level so it would take minimal site work, and it was easy to maneuver the trailer onto it.

It was an exciting day when we heard the roar of the big truck pulling our new home up the lane. There were several men helping to maneuver it so it didn't scrape on the uneven terrain. In the photo below you can see its final resting spot. Not exactly a beautiful object, but it was sweet to our eyes!

Once the trailer was set up level, on several piers to stabilize it, we turned our attention to the interior. One of the first things I did was to install a Franklin stove, a kind of wood-burning fireplace, so we would have enough heat to get us through the winter. This was a natural choice since we had an abundance of free firewood on our 70 acres. Such stoves are not particularly efficient, as we discovered, but it served the purpose.

I created a kind of hearth and surrounding wall around the stove by stacking bricks. This not only protected the area from the heat but provided thermal mass to help hold that heat and moderate the indoor temperatures. We also occasionally used a small portable electric radiant heater that you can see in the photo of Rosana to the right. We were both quite pleased to have this comfy new abode that seemed to be manifested almost instantaneously.

The double glass patio doors that came with the trailer were nice for great views and passive solar when the sun was shining, but I'm sure they were a net

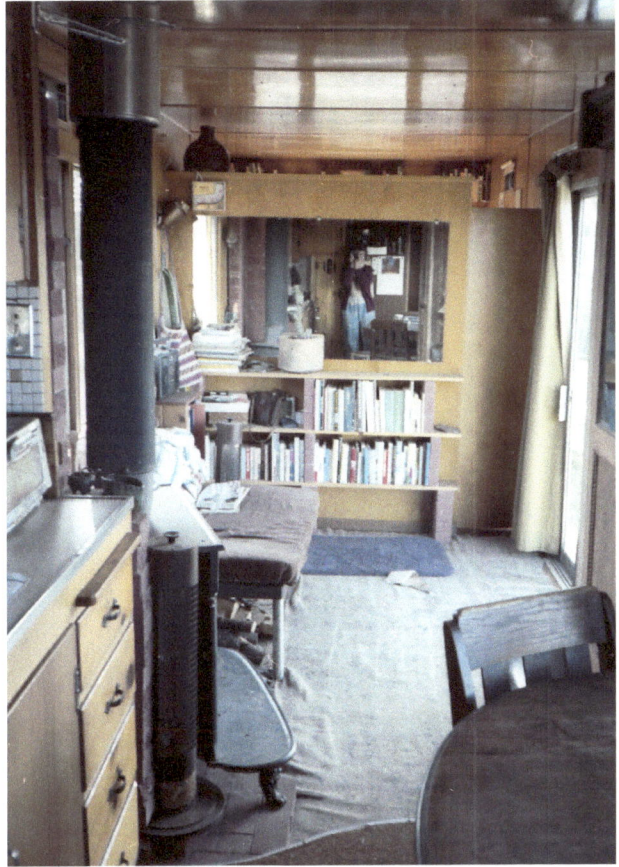

energy drain. We had a curtain we pulled across at night, but we would have been better off with some thicker insulating panels over those windows. I remember some mornings in the winter waking to find ice in the dog's water bowl, which was indoors.

This trailer had a bedroom at each end, and we used the one with a view of Mt. Shasta to sleep in; the other became Rosana's office. There was a large mirror on the dividing wall between the front bedroom and the living room, and the mirror enlarged the feeling of the space.

27

We got plenty of snow that first winter, and it would drift in some phenomenal ways, especially up near the crest of the ridge. The paved road was over a block away from where we were camped. They kept that road plowed to keep the ski resort open further up the mountain. But we were carrying water that first year so it was a burden to not be able to drive closer. We had already gotten a little all-wheel-drive Subaru wagon to replace the Mercedes, so we could at least get up to the entrance to our property. In the above photo you can just make out the Subaru buried by the snow when it was parked near the trailer. Our Rhodesian Ridgeback pup was lunging through the deep snow. I was getting around using a pair of home-made snowshoes. Van Corazon was totally snowed in and rather useless in the snow anyway, so we just left it there until spring.

We purchased an old Ford 9N tractor with a scraper blade on the back and a forked loader on the front. If the snow was not too deep I could run the tractor backwards and push it with the scraper blade. But for heavier snowfall, I attached a piece of plywood to the loader so I could actually scoop up snow and dump it off to the side. In this way we generally kept the driveway clear enough to drive most of the way to the trailer. That tractor was temperamental, though, and would not always start.

As challenging as all of this was, the sheer exhilaration of living in such a gorgeous place made life a pleasure. Every day we felt blessed by the opportunity we had to spend time there.

One December day before Christmas I was hiking along the ridge and noticed something bright red about a block away. At first I thought that perhaps a large kite or weather balloon had gotten caught in one of the trees, but as I drew closer I realized that it was a small plane that had crashed on our land. "Oh my God," I thought, "I hope nobody is hurt." That hope was dashed when I saw the pilot's head leaning out of the broken window and showing no signs of life.

I called the emergency number and soon the county sheriff and FAA authorities arrived to take stock of the situation. The body was taken away by ambulance. Later we learned from his brother that the pilot was quite experienced but had lately been taking inadvisable risks. He was probably trying to clear the pass in a thick fog without proper guidance equipment for low visibility.

We had a small ceremony with the brother and a friend of the pilot, burying his ashes at the base of the tree next to where he had crashed. I took the bent propeller from the plane and engraved his name and dates on it and mounted it on that tree. It seemed fitting for him to be buried in such a beautiful spot, right where he died.

We had hoped that we would have had our own water well established before winter hit, but the 440 foot well somehow got obstructed about half way down. The drillers had offered us the unusual deal that if they didn't produce water we would only pay a small fee for the attempt, so we weren't out a lot of money…just out of water.

I had found several small springs lower down on the property that I considered developing, perhaps with a hydraulic ram pump. This is a simple device that uses the power of falling water to force a small portion of that water back up a pipe quite some distance higher. I tried this in one location not too far from the trailer, and it worked marginally, but the spring stopped flowing in the dry months.

I was about to try pumping from a source down near the very bottom of the property quite some distance away, when it occurred to me that perhaps I should at least see if the dry well that was there when we bought the land was really dry. After all, a water witch whom we had hired to walk the land had said that there was a vein of water right near that old well. I cut through the welded seal at the top of the well and dropped a small stone down the hole.

"Splash!" Wow…that sounded like water. I lowered a weighted line down and found that there was about

50 feet of water in a well some 200 feet deep. Of course, any hole in the ground can fill with water over time, so the big question was "will it flow continuously when it is pumped?" The only way to find out for sure was to drop a pump down there and see what happened.

When I hired someone to try this we were amazed and delighted to discover that the well was actually producing about a gallon per minute. This is a minimal amount for many domestic scenes, but if you create a cistern to store water, it can be adequate. So we did just that, burying a concrete tank near the well, and plumbing the system so that it automatically kept the tank full and delivered pressurized water down to our home and garden.

Before we had moved to Oregon, Rosana had brought a book about llamas home from the library where she worked. Ever since then we had thought how neat it would be to actually own some llamas. Now that we had the space to do just that we got serious about finding some llamas to buy. One of the first we met was a young male appaloosa llama named Levi. We liked his looks and decided to buy him, along with his buddy Tumbleweed. It would be several months before they were old enough to be on their own and join us at Juniper Ridge.

In the meantime, we created some fenced areas and minimal shelter to house them. We thought that llamas would feel right at home in this mountainous area since their ancestral habitat was the high Andes in South America.

When the time came to go back to California, near where we used to live, to collect the llamas, I took Van Corazon. We were told that llamas are easy to transport in a van because they naturally hunker down, tucking their legs underneath themselves, to travel. This trip was especially exciting because I was also picking up my daughter who was coming for her first visit to Juniper Ridge.

The llamas and my daughter arrived in June and we had a surprise snowfall that month. We made a snow woman and my daughter named her "June Nipper."

It wasn't long before we bought other llamas to join Levi and Tumbleweed, including several females so we could do some breeding. This required more fencing and housing, both for the llamas and to store some hay for the wintertime. At this point we started calling the place Juniper Ridge Ranch, and made a sign to that effect at the entrance to our property.

In order to haul the hay, and for other tasks around the ranch, we exchanged Van Corazon for a 3/4 ton 4X4 pickup truck. So that we didn't lose our facility for camping trips, we also got a used camper that slipped into the back of the pickup. Now we were much better set up for the winters.

We had spent much of our savings getting set up with llamas, so we came up with a scheme for creating a much larger home that would utilize our existing trailer along with another of similar size. The concept was to park the two of them in the shape of a V with the wide open part of the V facing south. Then we could combine the two into one structure by building a roof over the whole affair, creating a large sun room in between the two trailers.

This would give us considerably more space and make the house much more comfortable with better insulated walls and solar heat. I conceived of making the back part of the central room with a raised floor, so that a bin of stones could be housed underneath. This would become a large duct that would store extra heat collected in the room, using a fan to force hot air from the top of the room down through the stones so it would recirculate.

We found another inexpensive trailer that was in good shape and parked it a lttile higher on the ridge. Then we moved the turquoise trailer nearby in that V shape.

In the photo below you can see the new arrangement of the trailers, as well as several llama sheds. You can also see the power line that was brought in earlier.

Another project for that fall was to put in a septic system and leach field to deal with our waste water.

This was located about 200 feet away in a field on the north side of that ridge, where there was soil that drained well.

Then I began construction of the central room. I cut some large cedar trees from our property to sink into the ground as pole supports for the roof structure. These are naturally rot resistant, but I also coated the buried parts with wood preservative. I left a few protruding branches that could be used to hang things on. You can see above that the trailer itself was stabilized with some concrete blocks. And lying on the ground was a long maple pole later used as part of the roof truss system.

Above, you can see that I had scraped the bark off the ends of the cedar poles that would be buried so that the wood preservative would sink in.

Below, the project was further along, with all of the cedar posts in place and the maple cross beams tied up there. A fair amount of stonework had been done, creating a floor for the front part of the sun room as well as a foundation and sill for the massive bay of windows that was to surround the front of that room. There was an opening for the front door. The window sill was made from rough 2X12 redwood slanted to shed water. Back then you could still get nice heart-wood redwood for such projects.

A couple of our lady llamas surveyed the scene.

In the above photo you can see how the framing for the entire structure began to take shape. The roof was to be metal, so the framing needed to provide support for that. The wings over the two trailers would eventually be supported by more cedar posts, but here one of them is just resting on a temporary board laid along the top edge of the trailer. I didn't want to rely on the trailers themselves to support any weight, especially with the kind of snow that we got.

Below is a good view of some of the framing details. The major trusses were bolted with threaded rod and there were actually two rafters that bridge the natural wooden braces and the top of the poles. The connecting pieces between the rafters were attached with joist hangers. The extension pieces that go out to the bay windows rest on a top plate and were long enough to provide some eave over the front. You can also see that the rafters that extend over the trailers were connected to the poles and interfaced with the upper rafters.

On one side we decided to make a carport area, so the roof was extended over far enough to accomplish that. You can see how the whole window bay was framed with the roof above it connecting it to the rest of the roof. Most of the glass was sliding glass door dual pane seconds that I picked up cheaply, so the spacing was set to approximately 3 foot widths.

33

The feeling of the interior space was beginning to be manifested at this point.

Below you can see how the roof wing over the trailer was supported by planted cedar poles. At this point the metal roofing had also been placed over most of the entire structure.

Next came the process of sealing up the whole space, as is shown in the photo on the right. The board and batten cedar siding was going on. But before the

siding went up an extra layer of inch and half EPS foam insulation was attached to the sides of the trailer to increase the insulation value of the shell. This insulation was extended down into the ground a way, and then metal skirting was placed over it to protect it from the elements. All of the windows were carefully framed with some of the same wood to provide sills and cover the foam insulation. Ultimately the only part of the trailer that was still visible from the outside was the tongue used to tow it, as you can see on the opposite page. Notice that I also made a rain gutter by cutting a large PVC pipe in half.

The above view is how the completed project looked.
I made the front door out of wood scraps and some
small thermal pane windows. The white things behind the glass were rolling thermal curtains to either
keep the heat in or to block the sunlight when it was
not welcome. The small rectangles at the base of
those windows were vents that could be opened for
air circulation. We made similar rolling shades that
could be lowered to cover all of the glass except for
the tiny triangular sections at the very top.

At the right is a view of the carport area and the other
side of that trailer. You can also see how the roof
looked from a higher angle.

Inside the central space I began constructing a raised floor that would bridge the two trailers. In the front, where the sun would shine on it, I had already made a cemented stone floor, using local stones that had a sufficiently flat surface. This was intended to be a durable floor that we could bring the llamas into on occasion. (Llamas typically only use their own dung piles and rarely make a mess inside.) It was also intended to be a heat sink for solar gain.

In a confined area about a yard wide between the floor joists, I made a channel that I filled with loose stones. This channel ran the whole length of the floor to the back of the house. At that point there was a duct created within the framing of the back wall that extended from the bin of stones up to the apex of the ceiling. Eventually there was a large fan installed near the top of the duct that would force warm air that would naturally rise up there down through the rock bin and into the trailers as well. This air would then exit out the front of the rock bin through a vent under the floor. Supposedly then, if enough warmth had been collected on sunny days, we could access this warmth just by recirculating the air through the system. As I recall this idea did seem to work, but it was not that easy to know for sure how well it worked.

We installed a marvelous wood stove made by a local inventor. This was precisely fabricated from quarter inch steel and featured a little oven with clear glass doors where we baked bread, pies, chickens, etc. It was designed to function with a down draft.

We started using that central space as soon as we could, so you can see that it became a living room before any paneling was done over the ugly trailer exterior.

I cut a new door through the side of the trailer in order to gain access, and I made a couple of steps up to it from the living space.

We used large book cases and some filing cabinets as a partial divider between the living space and the back utility space.

I filled all of the voids in the ceiling with batts of insulation right away, and then covered that with plastic until I had time to install wooden tongue and grooved ceiling material.

Since we were also making a living with our work in carpentry, film animation, teaching classes, selling llamas occasionally, etc., we could only make progress on the building project when we had the time and the money to do so.

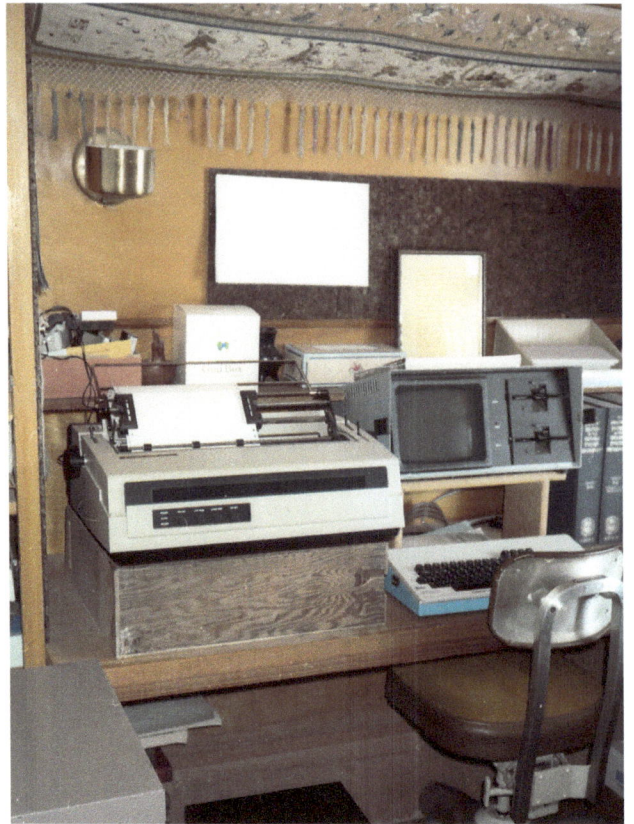

Directly through the door into the second trailer, on the opposite wall, I made a bin to store firewood so we wouldn't have to go outside so often to collect it. There was a pass-through door next to the wood pile, accessible from under the carport, so that we could just stack the wood from out there.

Rosana had her little office carved out of the tiny second bedroom in the first trailer, and you can see what that looked like above. The front room with the bay window in the second trailer became my office, which was nice since I had been making do with the Green Box. Below is a picture of this office.

The two photos above show how we converted the kitchen of the second trailer into a television viewing room and an editing space for my emerging work in videotape production. The extra bedroom in the back of the second trailer became Rosana's sewing room, guest space, and my daughter's room when she was visiting.

Below you can see the marvelous view we had out of our bedroom window.

One day we were paid a surprise visit by the county's Code Compliance Officer, who had noticed our construction when he was in the vicinity inspecting some other project. He said, "You know you need a permit to build an awning over a mobile home." I responded, "I thought I was just building a greenhouse." He disagreed and said he would send up an inspector to discuss it with us.

The inspector arrived the next day and told us that he couldn't approve it because it was not built to code. Then he said, "My boss can approve it, though, and don't worry because he will love it!"

Later, a dapper older gentleman came by and looked the situation over, with obvious interest. He wasn't sure about the truss system, but suggested that I set up a gauge to monitor any movement. Ultimately, all I needed to do was submit a plan for what I had done, along with the permit fee, and the county was content. I think I got off easy, considering what they could have demanded.

Below is a rough diagram of the floor plan of the house once we had finished all of the remodeling. It encompassed around 1200 sq. ft. and provided all of the amenities that made life good for us. We each had our own office space; we had a guest bedroom, with a second bathroom; there was plenty of space for exercising; there was a utility room with washer and dryer and a freezer; there were two dining spaces, depending on how many people were eating; there was a comfortable place to watch TV; there was a planter for growing produce year round; there were the stacks of our library (a fact that librarian Rosana really appreciated); and we even had a hot tub out in the sun room to soak in after a day of working on the ranch!

Not shown in the diagram is the convenient carport next to the second trailer, and as part of this, a large covered wood storage area…right next to where the wood could be passed through to the wood compartment on the inside.

With all of the insulation that surrounded the shell of the house it was much more comfortable and easy to heat than before. The sun room gathered a tremendous amount of heat during most days, and it was stored in all of the thermal mass to help keep things warmer at night.

This entire project only cost a few thousand dollars, plus a considerable amount of sweat equity.

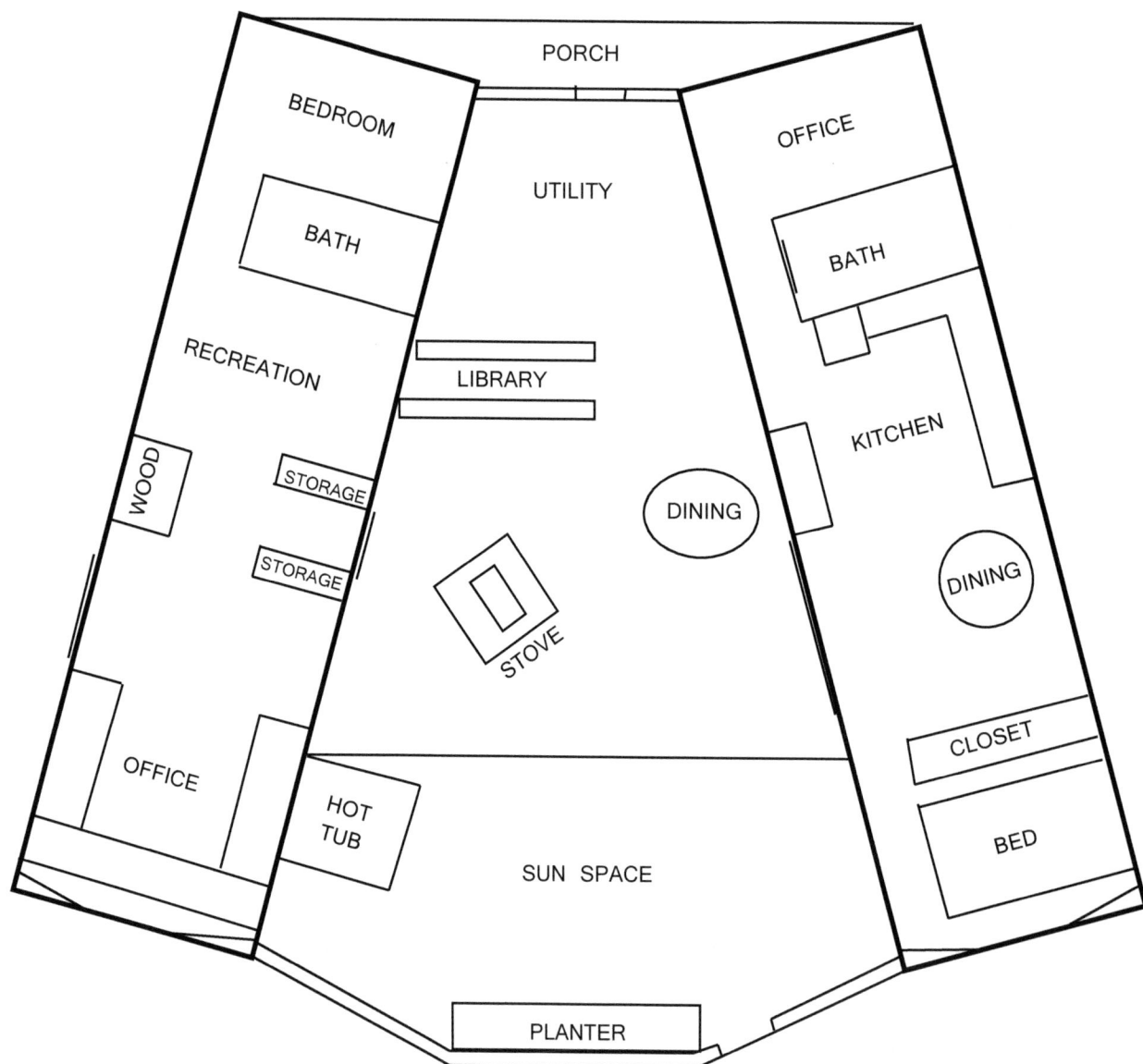

I designed some stained glass to fit in the little triangular sections above the main windows and commissioned my sister Molly, a stained glass artist, to execute them. I was very pleased with the effect. You can also see in the photos that I had finished the wood paneling on the ceiling.

There were some little vents up high on either side of the apex of the ceiling that were actuated by pulling ropes. This allowed some direct ventilation at the point where the heat would naturally collect.

Over the years that we lived on Juniper Ridge we increased our llama herd to as many as a dozen at any one time. We had several females that we bred, and we sold most of their offspring. We also had a collection of males that we used both for breeding and for a little packing business that we started.

Ashland is famous for its Shakespeare Festival, bringing many tourists to the area. We decided to capitalize on this by inviting some of them to visit

our ranch during the daytime and meet our llamas. We took them on picnic hikes, where the visitors would lead the llamas and the llamas would carry the picnic to some wonderful spots we had developed on the ranch. We never made very much money doing this, but it was a lot of fun to introduce people to these exotic animals. Below, Levi was looking over a picnic spread we had prepared.

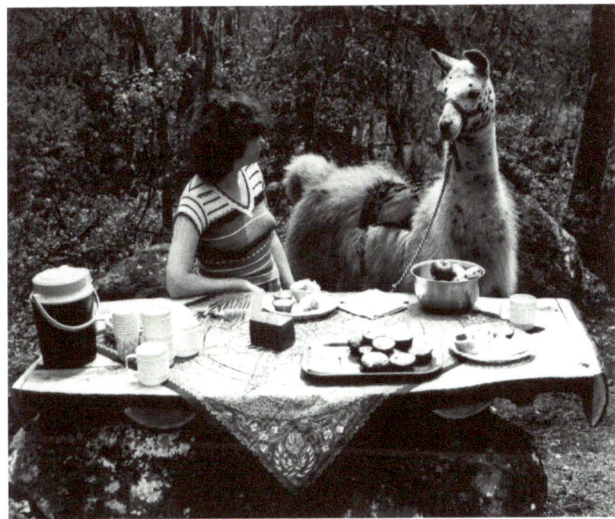

Rosana wrote a book about our experiences with llamas on Juniper Ridge. She titled this *Living with Llamas* and it went through four editions before going out of print; it can currently be downloaded as a free PDF at www.llamas-information.com.

I started producing video programs about llamas in general around the same time, and we combined these enterprises into a llamas information business that kept us busy.

We were early adopters of computers as you can see from the Kaypro "portable" computer that Rosana was writing on.

As time went on, we found ourselves more and more focused on our writing and video production, and developing these into our core business. The business of breeding and selling llamas was becoming less important to us and in some ways was a distraction from our ability to follow our instincts with the arts. I travelled to the Soviet Union to make some video programs, and we published several other books about llamas.

After seven years of living on Juniper Ridge we decided to board out the llamas with friends to give us more freedom. But then the idea of continuing to live on the ranch without the llamas didn't seem right; they were so intrinsically connected to the place in our minds. I had also begun to feel uneasy about living on such an obvious "power spot," much as Native Americans don't set up their camp in the places where they go to do vision quests. The fact that we had endured three plane crashes within about a mile of our place also weighed heavily on my mind. There was a kind of threshold for survival that I sensed.

In the end, we decided to sell Juniper Ridge and move on to other adventures.

Above, we are both wearing promotional sweat shirts, Rosana's featuring her book, and mine with the logo for our ranch and the llama hikes.

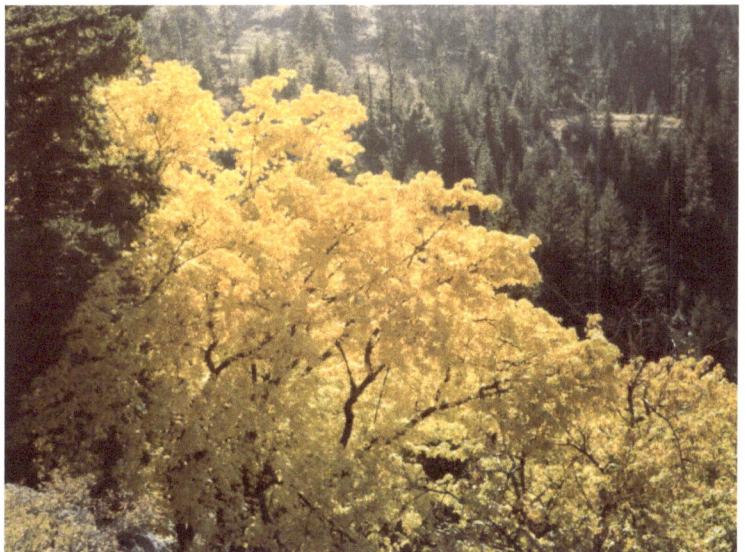

Tortuga & CanDo

We have owned two versatile RVs of about the same vintage. They were both early 1980's Dolphin motor homes, built on Toyota truck frames. These little gems provided all of the comforts of home. To us, they seemed better designed than many larger rigs, with all of the essentials conveniently arranged.

Since the coach and the driving compartment are all of a unit, there is a simplicity compared to towing a separate trailer. You can walk into the living part directly from the cab, making it very convenient. And since they were only about 20 feet long, they were easy to park or fit into a variety of camping spots.

They used the same four cylinder engine that the little Toyota trucks of the same era had, so they got surprisingly good gas mileage; we have averaged about 17 mpg with our Dolphins. Of course this means that they lacked power to zoom up hills, but we were rarely in a hurry when we were on the road anyway.

We called our first Dolphin "Tortuga," which means turtle in Spanish. Compared to some of our smaller campers (like Van Corazon or the VW Vanagon) these were definitely a step up in luxury. They featured a walk-in bathroom with sink, shower and toilet. The kitchen was fully functional, with lots of cabinets (both under counter and above), a sink with hot pressurized water, a four-burner cook top and a small oven. In addition there was a 3-way RV refrigerator built in; this could be operated either on propane, 12-Volt, or 120 Volt AC electricity…very versatile.

The main bed was up over the cab and could easily sleep two. You had to climb into this bed, but you could make up another bed at the other end of the coach by collapsing the table and rearranging the cushions. This meant that you could actually sleep up to four people inside, though we never did. There is even a small clothes closet with its own door.

What we especially liked about both of the Dolphins we have owned was that the layout placed the table and seats in a U-shaped pattern at the far end. There

are windows around this entire space, so when seated you have a great view of the scenery outside. We often would back the unit into a camp spot where we were looking out at a lake or river view, which felt very private.

We had Tortuga when we were living in Olympia, Washington, and enjoyed taking it to the Pacific coast. We bought a little camping lot about a block away from the beach and developed it so that we could park Tortuga at the base of the lot in a private nook (pictured above). From there we could either walk to the beach, or climb to the upper end of the lot where we could enjoy a nice view of the ocean.

These Dolphins were set up with dual tires on the rear axle, and the chassis was capable of carrying a full ton, twice what the original Toyota trucks could handle.

They were maneuverable enough that they could be parked on city streets, and we have often used them as our main mode of transportation, especially on long trips.

Each one had a small propane furnace that could keep the space quite comfortable, even in rather cold weather. We often camped for extended periods out in the boondocks, without plug-in electricity or water, since there was a fresh water tank for about 25 gallons, and both black and gray water tanks as well.

We added extra coach batteries to extend the time between needing charges, and with our second Dolphin, CanDo, we also added solar electric panels to the top to keep the batteries nicely charged most of the time, even when parked. We had a small inverter that would change the 12 Volt DC current to regular AC current so we could run small appliances or charge our computers.

On several trips into Mexico with CanDo, we equipped ourselves with a portable satellite internet system. It took some careful pointing of the dish to connect with the service, but since we were making our living via internet activities, it was essential for extended trips, especially when we were away from internet cafes, which was much of the time.

In the photo below you can see the internet satellite dish and the fixed ladder attached to the back that enables one to climb up on top to secure items for storage to a rack up there.

Below is a view of the kitchen arrangement taken from the seat next to the table. On the right were the stove, oven and refrigerator. We generally carried extra potable water, especially in Mexico. A simple pump arrangement fit into the water jugs to draw out water without our having to tip the jug. There was quite a bit of cupboard space on both sides of the RV.

Beyond the kitchen, you can see the bed in the cab-over loft. Under the bed was the opening for climbing into the cab for travel. We also used the cab for just sitting to read. One of our dogs loved being up front.

The photo on the right shows the double kitchen sink arrangement. It was small but serviceable. Just beyond the sink was the small closet door with a mirror on it. Out of view to the right of that was the bathroom. Below the towel rack was another potable water storage container. We used the large tank of pressurized water just for washing dishes, showering, and flushing the toilet.

Above, CanDo had the bed made up in the back, and below, that area was set up with the table and benches.

At right is the bathroom, with the toilet and shower stall next to it. We installed a number of baskets and holders for bathroom supplies. A little sink is out of view, inside the shower.

We made three long trips into Mexico with CanDo, and the above scenes are from these. Top left, we were parked on the Gulf of Mexico; top right was in an RV park in Guanajuato; bottom left was at the gate to Las Pozas; the last was the place where CanDo was based for nearly five years on property we bought near Lake Chapala. You can read Rosana's account of our life and travels in Mexico at www. mexicowithheart.com

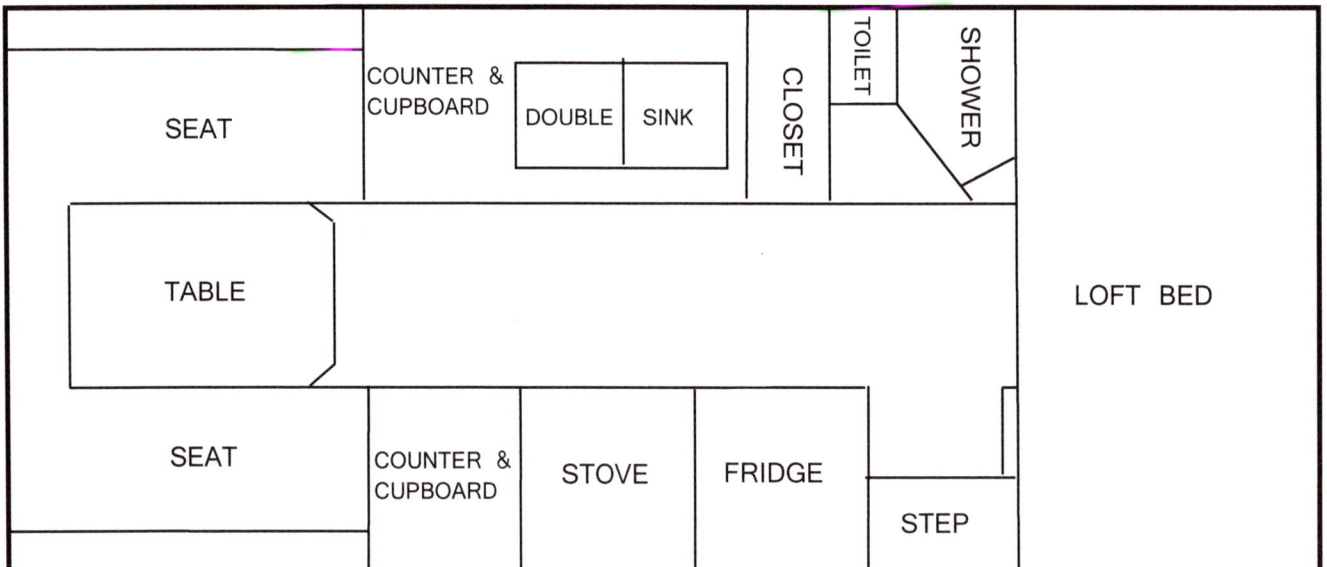

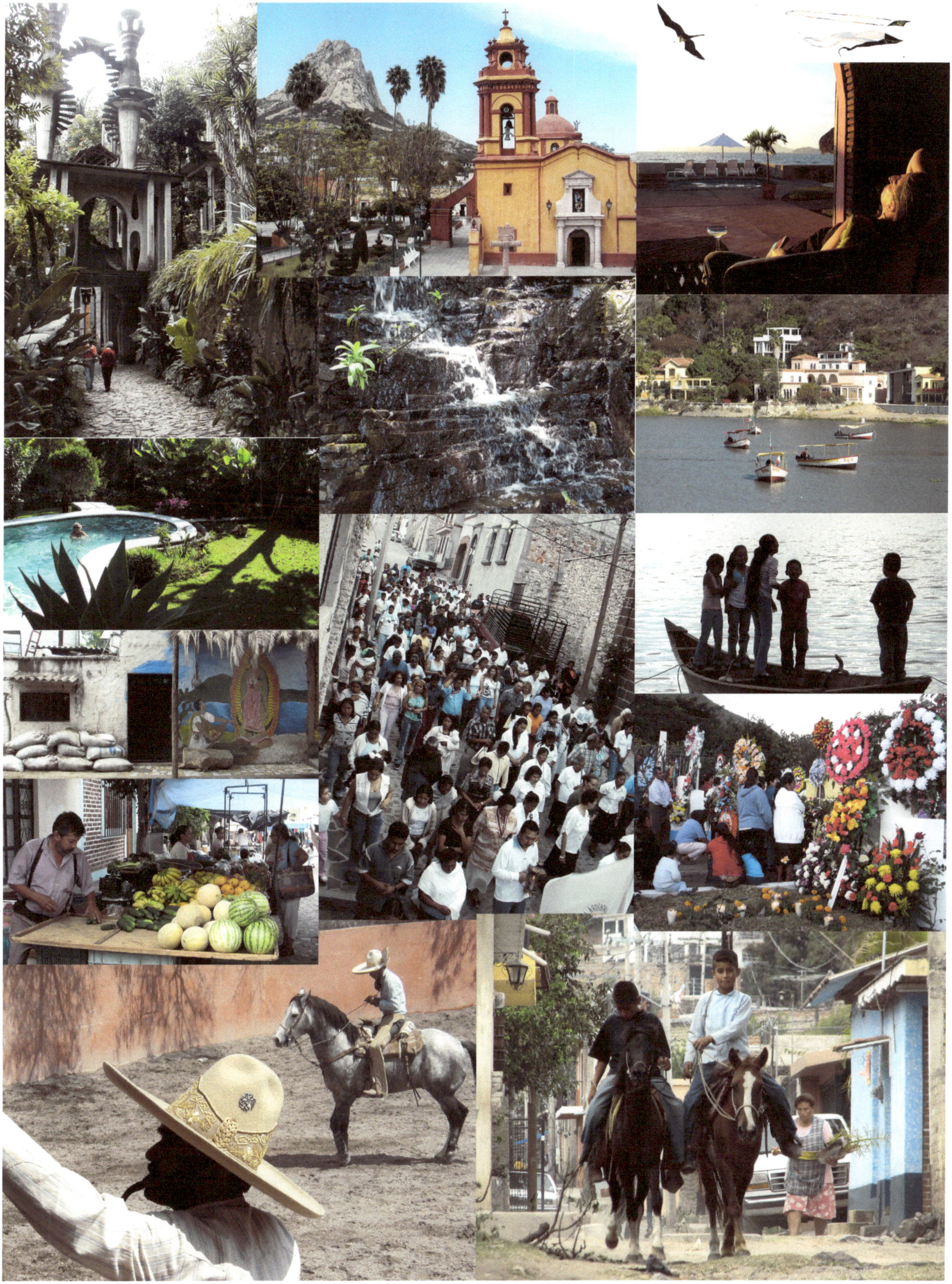

Here & There

After leaving Juniper Ridge we lived in the city of Ashland for a few years, then moved on to Olympia, Washington. Around this time we had Tortuga, as described in the last chapter. But after a few years living in a city, we developed severe wanderlust and started to think about having another big bus that we could live in full time and also drive from place to place.

Old buses come in many guises, some ugly and some quite nice, and of course there are many levels of mechanical soundness. We carefully researched what was available in the Olympia vicinity, and located a place in nearby Seattle where quite a few used buses were assembled for sale. An exploratory trip netted several possibilities, in terms of being affordable, having an appropriate configuration to convert into a motor home, and mechanical soundness.

The bus pictured above was of particular interest because it seemed to be in good shape, had a flat, level floor on the inside, and was plenty big…40 feet long with luggage bins under the floor, and it had a bit over 6 feet of head room inside. It had last been used as a tour bus in Hawaii, so it hadn't accumulated as many miles as many buses of its vintage. It was manufactured by Prevost, a well-respected Canadian bus company.

This was a bus that was designed to cross the country countless times, so it was very robust. Instead of being built on the sort of frame that most school buses and city transport buses use, these buses are built more like the way a bridge is built.

The engine (placed at the very back of the bus) was a huge 8 cylinder Detroit diesel, and the transmission was automatic, which meant there would be no double clutching, or constant changing of gears.

It was fitted with a full complement of seats and overhead luggage racks and even sported a microphone amplification system for the driver/tour guide to use. Another thing I liked was that all of the windows hinged open from the top, as a safety feature for emergency exits. This meant it would be easily ventilated.

Since I am not a diesel bus mechanic, I needed an expert's opinion about the condition of the bus before I offered to buy it. So I found a shop that specialized in working on buses that was not far away from where the bus was stored, and the company that was selling it agreed to let them drive it to their facility where they could drive it over a pit for a thorough inspection.

The bus passed this inspection with flying colors, so we paid the asking price of about $18,000, and the bus was ours. I actually traded all of the bus seats as part of the fee for inspecting the bus, which was convenient, since I had no use for them. What a thrill it was to drive such a beast home to our back yard in Olympia. Now I had my work cut out for me!

Though you may not have the interest, time, or skills to do what I did to convert a bus into a home, I will go into some detail about how I did it; this may provide some inspiration for what can be done.

Above, the bus was parked in our back yard, and I was digging into one of the luggage bays. There was a large air conditioning system that I removed to make more room for storage beneath; we planned to install a small evaporative cooler for the coach and didn't need this elaborate system.

The bus rode on air bags for a suspension while in motion, but when parked it settled down low to the ground, as you can see in the above photo.

The massive diesel engine was fairly easily accessible to work on. We didn't know it at the time, but this model engine was notorious for splattering oil when in use; there was even a dedicated slobber tube that just spilled the excess oil out onto the ground (or anything that might be towed behind it).

On the left side of the bus you can see one of the windows propped open for ventilation. We added screens to these openings to keep insects out. We made these from screen material, sewing velcro to the screen and gluing it to the window frame.

One of the first things I did when tackling this project was to establish a work station for assembling tools and supplies and to use as a work bench. I did this at the front of the bus because my plan was to start at the very back with the remodel and work my way forward. I even had a small table saw to help with milling lumber.

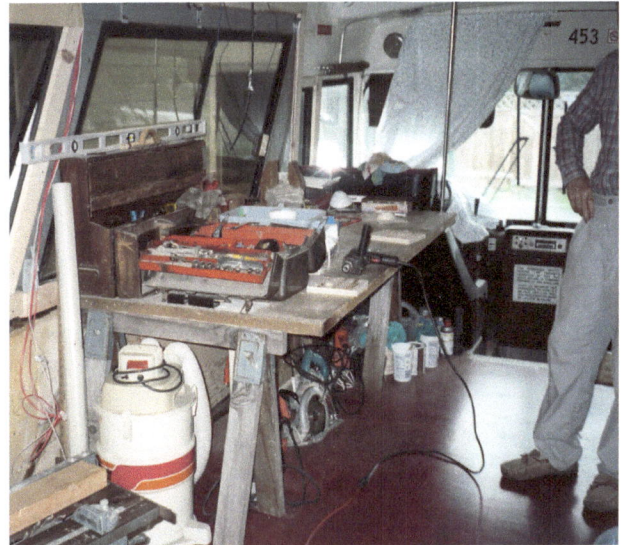

Right away I stripped all of the interior paneling off of the walls and ceiling. I did this for several reasons: I planned to add more insulation in these areas (in addition to the foam insulation the factory had sprayed in between all of the framing members) and use other materials for the paneling. I also wanted to expose the entire space in order to place wiring circuits behind the paneling.

So for this I needed to have a master plan for wiring the bus; this was an elaborate project, since it involved both AC and DC circuits.

51

I needed to know exactly where all of the electrical circuits would go, which meant knowing what appliances I expected to install and what their electrical needs would be.

My plan was to mount solar panels on the roof of the bus, which would charge a bank of batteries housed in one of the luggage bays. From there 12 volt electricity would be available, and all of these circuits were routed through a fuse box (pictured above). I would also install an inverter to supply 120 volt AC current, and this would be placed near the batteries. All of the AC circuits would be routed through a standard breaker box, as pictured to the right.

Appropriate wire sizes needed to be calculated, based on the current they were expected to carry and the length of the wire. In a moving vehicle it is highly recommended to use stranded copper wire rather than the solid copper wire typically used in house wiring. This is because it is much more pliable and less likely to break due to vibrations over time.

Below you can see how I precut all of the wire and placed it in the areas where it needed to be routed.

The ceiling circuits included lights and switches, vent fans and evaporate coolers. Lower down were all of the standard outlets, propane heater fans, compost toilet fan, etc.

To know where all of this stuff should be I carefully drew an outline of the floor plan directly on the floor of the bus. That way I could place fuse and breaker boxes where I knew they would be safe and accessible. This floor plan was designed well in advance of any significant construction, and can be seen on the next page.

The wood framing around the windows and at the base of the wall was there to provide space for the 3/4 inch insulation I would be adding. Also, it provided something to easily anchor the eventual interior paneling to.

Floor Plan (diagram labels)

- DRIVER'S SEAT
- STEP
- STEPS
- SWIVELING RECLINER
- DOOR
- DESK & STUDIO
- SOFA BED
- SINK
- SINK
- HEATER
- KITCHEN COUNTER
- TABLE
- STOVE
- FRIDGE
- SHOWER
- PANTRY
- DOOR
- SINK
- HEATER
- TOILET
- FILES
- DESK
- DOOR
- DESK
- HEATER
- BED
- CLOSET

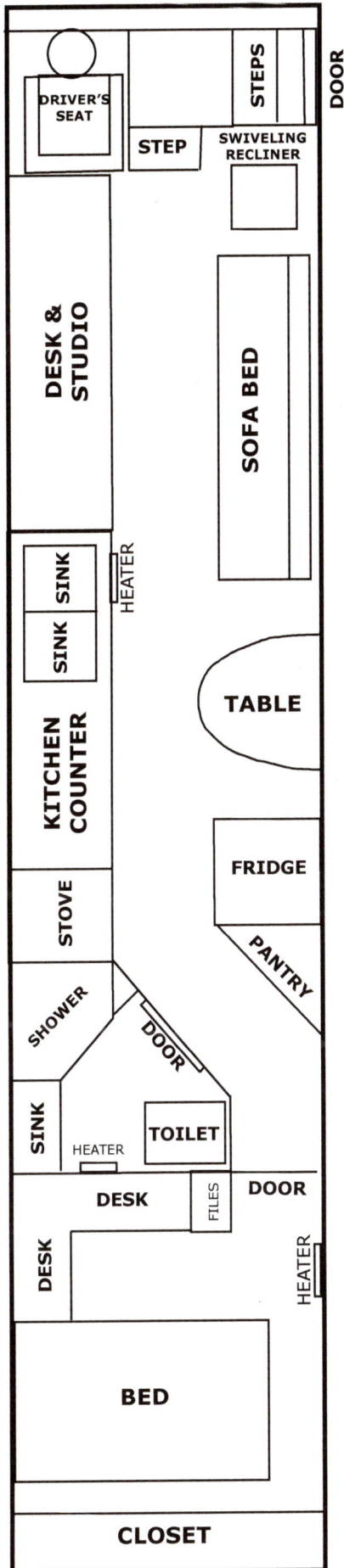

Since the bus was eight feet wide, there was no avoiding some sense of having a corridor that runs the length of the bus. We diminished this effect somewhat by angling the pathway at the point where the bathroom starts, at the end of the kitchen. We also provided some privacy by placing a door into the bedroom/office space. In addition we arranged the bathroom door in such a way that it could be left open, in which case it could be latched up against the pantry. This would in effect create a private bedroom suite that included the bathroom.

With the two desk arrangements at either end of the bus, Rosana and I could both be working on projects independently without unduly disturbing the other. We are both self-employed and work at home, so this was essential.

The back of the bus would be our bedroom and Rosana's office space. The area where there used to be a bench across the back would become a closet. Beneath that bench frame was the engine compartment, so I couldn't really alter that. In fact there was a little door that accessed part of the engine, and I left that intact as well.

In the above photo, all of the areas that were painted grey were steel framing members that had rusted some, I expect from condensation in the humid Hawaiian climate. I had gone through the entire bus and treated all of the rusty spots in a similar manner. The things assembled along the ledge in the closet are there to see what would fit in that space. In vehicle living it is important to utilize every bit of storage space available.

The above photo shows a lot about how I remodeled this bus. At the very back was the closet before the doors were put in. All of the shelving in there was salvaged from the interior luggage racks; the bottom shelves were designed for shoes, leaving enough space on the left for long clothes to hang. The clothes hanging rod was a stainless steel pipe recycled from the front of the bus where it had been something to hang onto as people entered the bus. The paneling behind the shelves and coming forward along the sides was a tough quarter inch hardboard with a baked enamel paint. On the left below the windows was natural 3/8th inch cedar tongue and groove wood; I chose this to give the sense of old-fashioned wainscotting.

Both on the ceiling and on the sides 3/4 inch foil-backed foam insulation was added before the paneling was attached. The ceiling paneling in the bedroom was natural birch quarter inch plywood, something that looked great when lying in bed and gazing upward. The hole in the ceiling is for one of the powered RV vents that would automatically close itself if rain were detected.

The base of the closet enclosure was lined with more of the birch plywood. The two patches to the original red linoleum floor were made with 1 inch plywood. This was necessary because the wheel wells beneath there had rotted out the original flooring, with all of the water thrown up there over the years. (I also lined those areas with sheet metal under the floor in an attempt to avoid further damage.)

On the left you can see the wall-mounted direct vented propane catalytic heater, and above it over the window was the thermostat control for this heater.

The aluminum bars at the base of each window were the release catches that allowed the windows to swing outward at the base. To finish the windows, I used L-shaped wooden molding. The junction between the ceiling panels and the side panels was finished with some specially milled molding as well. The windows themselves were a dark-tinted automotive glass that gave the interior a lot of privacy during the day. At night we pulled curtains across the windows, and when it was cold, we put in insulating reflective panels.

I had one of the windows propped open for air. Eventually each window had special hardware that would hold it open. One nice thing about this arrangement is that the windows could actually be left open in a light rain and no water would enter since the glass naturally shed the rain away.

The next process in this project was to begin laying the oak flooring. I found some reasonably priced tongue and grooved flooring that had been finger jointed, with several short pieces combined into longer boards. Making the job easier, it had also been pre-finished. In the photo below you can see how I installed this flooring in the bedroom before I began work on the bed platform.

Above, the sliding closet doors had been installed, using some nice 3/4 inch birch plywood. They hung on a track that allowed each of the two doors to slide past the other, depending on which side you wanted to access. Also, you can see that the ceiling vent had been installed. This vent had a thermostatically controlled fan and a motorized crank to raise the top.

The bed platform was composed of a large dresser that I cut in half and used as a support on either side, with drawers providing storage in both directions. The platform itself was 3/4 inch plywood coated with urethane. We used the little slots under the platform to store the insulation panels for the windows. There was also some extra storage space for larger items under the head of the bed and between the dresser parts.

The above photo was taken after we had begun to move into the bus, so the bed is in place. We added a mirror to the sliding closet door, curtains over the windows, a ceiling light, and an insulated cap for the ceiling vent. Later still, we added an evaporative cooler to the ceiling and a cabinet over the bed.

After getting the bed in place, I turned my attention to adding the little office nook for Rosana. But before I could build anything in that space, I needed to assemble the structure for the wall that would separate that space from the bathroom. This was a simple wall framed with 2 X 4's oriented so that the wall would only be about 2 inches thick. For this wall, I used a quarter inch hardboard that had an interesting stone-like pattern on it.

We used a wooden two-drawer filing cabinet that we happened to have to help support the little desk. And the side extension of the desk was attached to the bed for support. Underneath that extension we carved out space for a crate for our basenji pup.

I added more shelving and cabinets into that space, making it fairly functional as an office, if tiny. The antlers near the ceiling were added after we found them on a hike, and were used to hang necklaces, etc. Built-in trays for organizing papers and other supplies were above the filing cabinet. Besides the regular outlet for AC electricity, there was a 12 Volt DC plug on the wall.

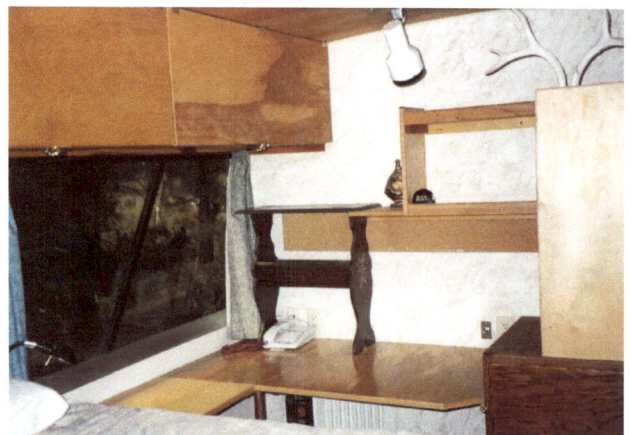

At his point I could turn my attention to the bathroom itself. I had purchased a commercial corner shower pan with the entrance fashioned diagonally from the corner. I used this pan to position the exact location of the walls around it. I found a fun hardboard paneling that was printed with a tile pattern that was quite realistic and would be easy to keep clean.

I insulated the bathroom walls with rigid insulation in an attempt to keep the sound of the vented compost toilet fan from being heard in the rest of the bus. In the photo you can see the sink waiting to be installed. Also visible is the white vent pipe running up alongside one of the wall studs; this pipe vented the grey water holding tank located beneath the bathroom in one of the luggage bays. The ceiling panelling over the rest of the bus would be the white hardboard shown above.

At the right is how the finished bathroom turned out, with the shower stall next to the vanity. We mounted a shower curtain onto a curved section of copper pipe.

I tiled the floor of the bathroom with dark marble. It was fairly expensive, but since it was such a small space I didn't need much. That is one of the nice things about outfitting a small space: you can lavish a bit of luxury here and there without breaking the bank.

Instead of a common RV flush toilet we decided to install a compost toilet (pictured to the right). This is generally a more ecological option for dealing with human waste and I had had experience with one before. We chose a Sun-Mar brand toilet that was designed for tight spots, like in a boat. It was rated for two people to use, had a powered vent to keep any fumes to a minimum, and even had an electric heater to help with the composting action if necessary.

We used this toilet for a number of years, and it is one of the few appliances we installed that we weren't very happy with. Despite it being designed for two people to use, we overwhelmed its capacity with our regular use. Perhaps they didn't expect full-time use. In any case it did require emptying occasionally before the waste was fully composted…and that was no fun!

Outside the bathroom I continued the wainscot motif with the cedar and installed a door made from birch plywood. There was an odd triangular space between the shower stall and the angled wall of the bathroom which I devoted to spice shelves for the kitchen at the top, and bathroom storage on the bathroom side at the base.

The paneling that surrounded the stove was more enameled hardboard that would be easy to keep clean. There was one of the bus windows that I completely blocked off, since I didn't want glass behind the stove or bathroom.

In the above photo you can see the kitchen cabinetry under way, with both overhead cabinets and counter with sink and drawers beneath. The counter was also

a cutting board made from solid birch, and the over-head cabinet was made with 3/4 inch birch plywood mounted very securely to to ceiling and wall.

Over the stove was a special range hood for RVs that featured gauges to monitor the fresh and gray water tanks. In addition I mounted a gauge to monitor the photovoltaic panels and battery system.

Over the sink we created a dish draining arrangement that would allow us to drain clean dishes directly into the sink in such a way that the dishes could actually stay there much of the time (except when we were traveling).

The hinged doors that accessed the space under the sink also sported a direct-vented propane heater. The idea with the swinging heater was that it could then be pointed in a variety of directions, including toward my office space just beyond the kitchen. Catalytic heaters are radiant, which means that they immediately heat objects that are directly in their path. This concept worked very well in practice. The thermostat for this heater was mounted on the panelling near the ceiling above it.

I used the same cedar tongue and groove wood I had put up for the wainscot as cabinet doors and drawer fronts. This tended to unify the overall appearance of the bus.

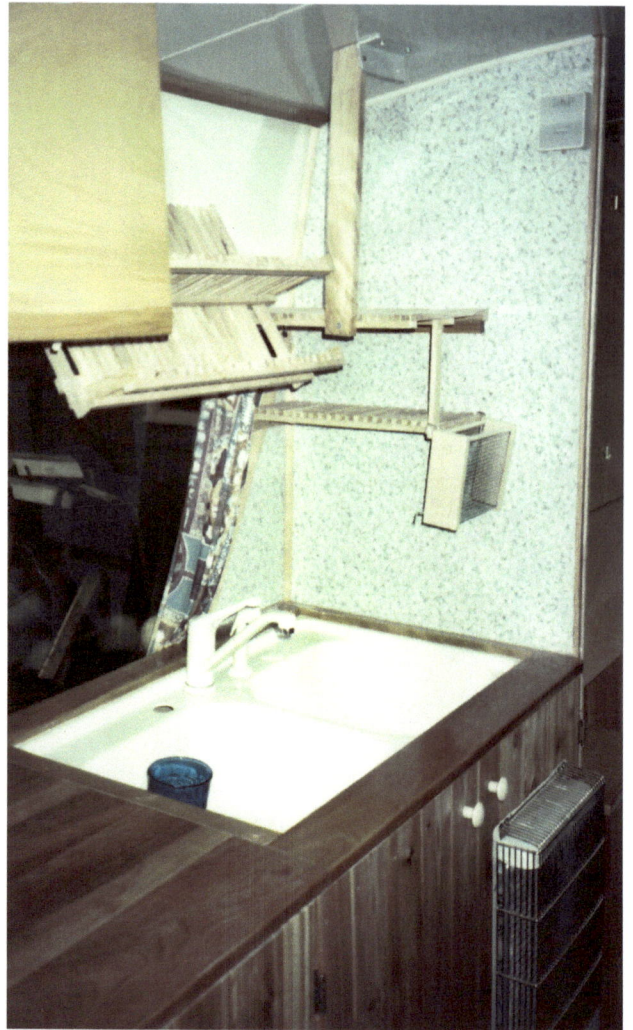

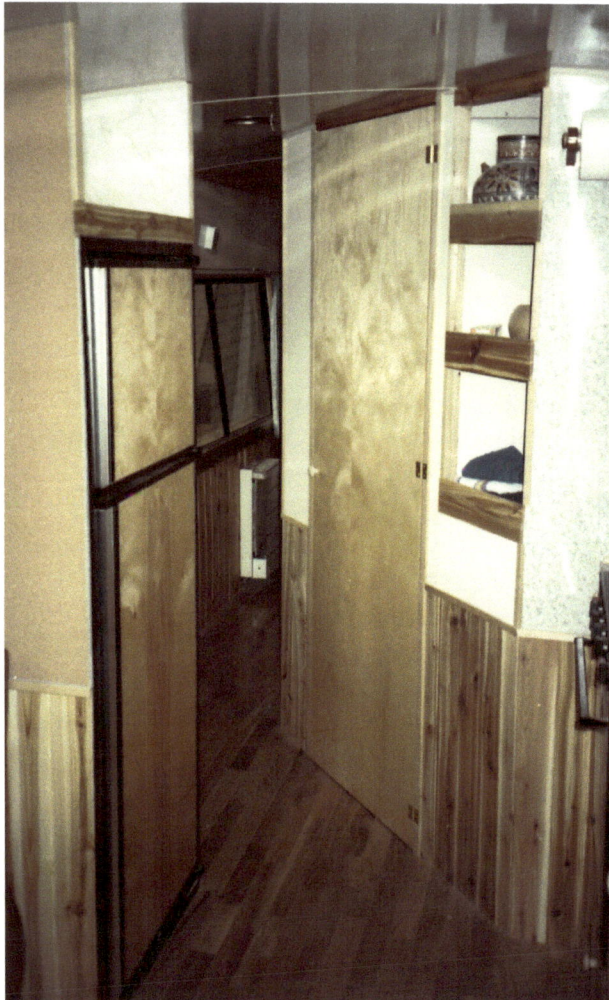

On the other side of the isle from the kitchen stove I built a cabinet to house the large RV refrigerator. This was a combination AC/DC electric or propane unit, and required special venting out the back. Above the fridge was a large storage compartment with a lip on the shelf to keep items from sliding off. The same principle was used on the spice shelves on the other side.

Around the corner from the refrigerator was an odd triangular space going down the hall that we turned into pantry shelving, with a secure door. There was even a second little door that opened to a tiny vertical space, just big enough to keep a broom. Of course this became our "broom closet."

The above photo shows what the finished kitchen/ dining area looked like. It turned out to be one of the best kitchen arrangements we've ever cooked in, with all necessary supplies and functions close by. And with that large cutting board/counter, there was plenty of space for chopping and assembling food. There was adequate drawer and cabinet space for all of the typical implements and supplies.

The oak dining table is one that we had owned for years, a French antique with a lot of personality. Unfortunately there wasn't room for the entire oval table, and I was torn by whether to cut part of it off in order to fit it into the bus; desecrating a fine antique is not something that I would do lightly. In the end, we decided to cut off a bit of one end, including two of the lovely fluted legs. So then the sliced end was firmly mounted to the side of the bus, and the result-ing dining

area was quite charming. I eventually gave the other cut end to a friend who placed it in a similar way in a miniature cabin he was building in the woods, so then the table had two lives!

The stained glass lamp over the table dated back to our first bus and was acquired by trading a pair of sheepskin slippers I had made with a local artisan who made the lamp. On the upper part of the refrig-erator cabinet was a large cork board for displaying artwork, etc. Mounted high above the table was a shelf for books, again with a retaining lip around the edge.

Most of the lights in the bus were 120 Volt AC compact fluorescent ones; these were actually more energy efficient than had they been DC lights that wouldn't have given off as much light. Nowadays, LED lights would be even better.

Between the driver's seat and the kitchen, I created a complex of cabinetry for my office and video editing suite. The desk itself hinged down, as you can see in the above photo. The racks above it were mostly for the electronics, plus some drawers. To the left of the desk was a filing cabinet that I faced with the cedar wood. Hinged almost out of sight to the right above the driver's seat was an accordion pleated and swinging cover for the upper part of the whole affair.

Whenever we drove the bus, or if I wasn't working at my desk and just wanted to simplify the appearance, we could close up the whole cabinet by quickly hinging up the desk and folding the upper panels across. The panels and desk locked firmly in place, effectively securing all of that equipment from jostling while we were in motion. If I needed a little desk space, I could just fold that part down, as pictured below.

Here you can see what it was like with all of the equipment assembled. The racks were completely adjustable, so it was quite a versatile space. I produced and edited several video programs at this station, including *A Sampler of Alternative Homes* (which included the bus), and the setup was quite functional.

Our living room was completed by adding a specially designed RV sofa and recliner. The sofa easily converted into a bed for guests, and we positioned it in such a way that one person could sit sideways and dine at the table. Underneath the sofa was room to store extra bedding. This was a comfortable spot to relax and watch TV or read. The living room and dining room combined to provide a relatively good space for socializing.

We could make the living area quite private by pulling curtains along the windows as well as placing Reflectix insulation panels over the windshield.

The recliner swiveled on its base, allowing the chair to face any direction. This enabled us to use it as a passenger seat while we were driving. We installed a seat belt to make this safe.

Beyond the recliner, you can see how we finished the entrance to the bus with the same cedar wood motif. Above the main bus door we had some hooks to hang wet coats so they could drain onto the step and not drip on anything.

Over the windshield outside the bus was a place for a marquee destination sign. When we bought the bus it just said CHARTER, but we wanted to put a name for our bus up there instead. We thought about this for a long time, and finally decided to name it HERE & THERE, since our intention was to go meandering without any particular destination in mind.

I built a bike rack for the front of the bus that would accommodate two bicycles.

Next to the recliner I put light switches that were easily operated when you first entered the bus. And then there was the oddity that the front door handle was built into the frame around the door rather than into the door itself. We needed a lockable latch for the door which was unfortunately too thick for the latches that I could find, so this was my solution. Once you got used to using it this worked quite well. A security latch when we were inside the bus was the standard levered door opener that could be operated from the driver's seat and locked in a closed position.

The luggage bays under the bus floor were a valuable asset for this conversion and they were fully utilized. Below, I was working on the water system.

Pictured above was a complex grouping of systems that took many days to assemble properly. Primary among these were the water systems, both fresh water and gray water. The three large holding tanks were made for this kind of bus conversion. They were behind everything else visible above and also show from the other side of that bay below. Each one held about 175 gallons, and two of them were devoted to fresh water, so the total capacity for fresh water was about 350 gallons. The third tank was for gray water. Below you can see the two filling spouts on the top of the two fresh water tanks. These spouts swiveled out in order to fill the tanks with a hose.

The water tanks were firmly held in place on the sides by rigid blueboard insulation; underneath them was plywood resting on more insulation. In fact, the entire enclosure was insulated, with both doors and the roof done as well. I had placed similar insulation under the main floor of the bus by wedging pieces between the framing members of the roof of every luggage bay. This was done to thermally isolate the living area.

On the left, in the above photo, was the valve and connection for dumping the gray water tank, as well as a valve for fresh water outside the bus. There was also a way to connect a hose to the plumbing to pressurize the system with another source of water when convenient. Above the valves was a pressure tank to keep the pump from cycling too frequently. In a separate box on the right was a standard RV water heater that was vented to the outside with louvered vents built into the hatch of the luggage bay. Directly above the water heater was the inverter for the photovoltaic system. Also visible was some of the plumbing for drains and water lines. This bay was directly below the shower, so you can see the P-trap for the shower. Under the bus was a place to plug in "shore power" for AC instead of using the on-board system.

Another luggage bay was devoted to miscellaneous tools and propane tanks. On the left in the above photo was the end of a propane tank that holds about fifty gallons and on the right was one that holds ten, which was the reserve tank if the main one was empty. There was a switching valve to go between the two tanks mounted on the roof of the bay. We used propane for catalytic heaters, the kitchen range, the refrigerator, and the water heater.

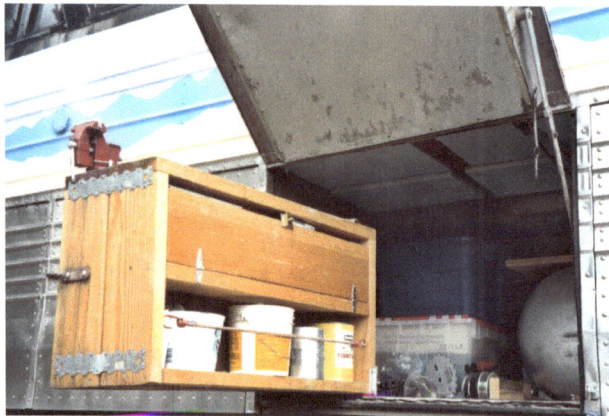

On the other side of that same bay I built a swivelling work bench that I could pull out to work at. It even had a small vise mounted on top. Neatly stored both inside the work bench and in plastic bins behind it were more tools and supplies. This whole arrangement was enormously useful for maintenance and little projects while on the road.

One such project was adapting a small used holding tank for use as a reservoir for collecting excess liquid that would drain out of the compost toilet, which was what I was doing in the photo to the right. Also vis-

ible in that photo was the little bay that housed both the bus battery (24 Volts) and the batteries for the solar electricity system (12 Volts). The solar panels for this system were mounted on the roof of the bus in such a way that they generally laid flat, so that we could safely travel. If we were parked for awhile, and the bus were oriented correctly, I could angle them toward the sun to gain a little more production of electricity.

This left two whole bays available to store all kinds of belongings and household supplies, which we put mostly in plastic bins that were carefully organized and labeled as shown on the opposite page. We had locks on all of the luggage bays for security, keyed alike for convenience.

Finally, after about a year of concentrated work, the bus was ready for travel, and so were we! While on the road we finished a number of projects that made the bus more comfortable. One of these was the fabrication and mounting of special lightweight shades that could be hinged out over the windows to keep the bus from getting too hot from sunshine. I had a long pole with a hook on it that I could use to bring the shades out or put them back tight against the top of the bus. These shades were made from light wood or PVC pipe frames with a blue awning fabric attached to them.

In addition to these shades, I mounted a used RV awning, complete with the aluminum hardware, on the side of the bus where my work bench was. Then I was able to work out there in most any weather. In the photo to the right you can see how this awning rolled out and was supported in that position with struts attached toward the side of the bus. Also visible in that photo are the solar electric panels and the two evaporative coolers mounted on the roof.

The picture below shows how that awning nested tightly against the bus when not in use. The setting of that photo is one of the early camping spots we found and demonstrates what exotic and wonderful places can be called home when travelling this way. We traveled with our two dogs and were basically free and footloose for the several years that we were full-timing in HERE & THERE. We had rented out our house in Olympia, Washington and had hired someone to fill orders for our book and videotape business.

Eventually we got tired of driving a bus labeled Hawaii, so I decided to paint a mural that would surround most of the bus instead.

We roamed around in the bus, mostly in the Western states, parking in RV campgrounds, state parks, Forest Service land, family and friends' land, often staying for weeks at a time if circumstances were right. The above photo was taken on some land that we bought very cheaply at a tax auction near Deming, New Mexico. We had the idea that we might develop several such parking spots in a variety of locales over time, and rotate among them. Life in the bus was very comfortable.

One of the places we visited and fell in love with was a small community high in the Sangre de Cristo mountains of south-central Colorado. We discovered that land in the area was quite cheap, so we bought a lot there as well. This would make a good contrast in climates, since it was over 8,000 feet in the mountains, with harsh winters, whereas the land in Deming was closer to 4,000 feet high.

Unfortunately, the rules of the property owners association controlled what could be done on the Colorado land, so we were not able to just park the bus on our lot for very long. They required that you actually be building a house on your land if you wanted to park an RV or camp there.

After awhile we decided to build an experimental earthbag domed house on that land, both as an experience in building such a house, and as an excuse for parking our bus home there. Another book in this series chronicling all of the different homes that I have built or modified is devoted to describing this unusual earthbag home.

Afterword

When I look back at the many years we have spent living in vehicles I am reminded of how much pleasure and stability it has given us. Pleasure from all of the wonderful experiences afforded by spending time in so many amazing and beautiful places. Stability from having a place to live in that is my own, that is paid for, and has all of my basic needs covered. I consider these things to be true wealth.

Obviously, using vehicles as a basic shell can take many forms, and what I have shown here are just a few of the possibilities; your imagination can conjure up many more. The main ingredient to make something like this work in your life is a willingness to dream about the possibilities and then to find a way to manifest that dream.

What has made it possible for me to take on the challenge of building homes out of vehicles is that early in my life I developed the skills and belief necessary to take on construction projects of all sorts. I learned a lot about carpentry from my father who was a part-time wood worker by trade, so that helped. I also inherited from him some basic skill sets that allowed me to believe that I could build most anything, if I put my mind to it.

I would encourage everyone to try your hand at making things as early in your life as you can, and teach your children to do the same. There is nothing more valuable for finding a way in life that is satisfying, economical, and sustainable, than developing these skills. This has often provided a livelihood for me, as well as enabling me to manifest the exact life style and surroundings that I find enriching. It is a way to follow your bliss!

One of the obvious advantages of rolling shelter, from the point of view of stainability, is that it is really light on the land; tire tracks don't last very long. Once a vehicle is moved from one location to another, there is no concrete foundation or supportive infrastructure left behind.

I have lost track of what happened to the first bus that I made into a home, as it was sold along with the property at Sunshine Camp, and I have not been back there to see. It could easily still be there and in use, since the shell was virtually indestructible aluminum.

Some of the smaller vehicles I lived in might have found their way to a wrecking yard or been crushed for recycled steel by now…it is hard to say. At the very least they served us during the time they were in our possession; none of them were new when we bought them, so they did not contribute to the stream of manufacturing new products and therefore have that distinction of being green.

In the case of the trailers that became part of the house at Juniper Ridge, I did return to that idyllic spot recently, after being away for over twenty years. We had sold the land to a couple from California who had rented out our old house.

I didn't know what to expect when I went back with a good friend who lives in the area. Well, the surprising thing was that the house was almost entirely gone! The only thing left was the stone masonry for the front of the sun room and the pile of stones that had served as thermal mass under the floor. In the photo below a couple of the outbuildings that I had built for the llamas can be seen in the distance, and that was about all that was left of that rich time in our lives.

At first I was shocked, after having devoted so much enthusiasm and energy into that building project, to find that it had vanished to that extent. There was no sign of fire, so obviously the whole scene had been deconstructed and the trailers likely hauled away. But as I talked it over with Rosana we realized that this was actually preferable to discovering that the place was totally trashed and derelict. Maybe the materials that had been accumulated to build it were now finding some other use. And even if this weren't the case, then at least the land at Juniper Ridge is now nearly back to its pristine quality.

But human life does continue at Juniper Ridge, since I did notice that just above the cliffs, on a separate parcel of land that we had sold along with the main one, was a new house.

It took us three years to build the earthbag house in Colorado, and during that time we were happily living in HERE & THERE. The first winter we drove down to New Mexico, but after that we stayed put, continuing the building. Even in this cold climate we were comfy enough in the bus.

In 2000 we were ready to move into our new house (shown above), which was a liberating experience after all of those years living in the confined space of a bus. Suddenly HERE & THERE was mostly here and stationary, as we became more engaged in our new life. We rented it out as a small dwelling for a while, but then decided to sell it. We advertised it and eventually I even drove it to a bus conversion consignment yard in Arizona, but people seemed to be put off by the compost toilet, and other unconventional aspects. In the end, after more than a year, we sold it to some friends for a greatly discounted price. It was

driven to California and Oregon and became living space for an electrician when he was in the field with his work. Now it is back in our same community and we see it occasionally.

While we were living in the earthbag house, we started getting wanderlust again, and that is when we bought CanDo, our second Dolphin motorhome, and started taking it to Mexico on a variety of excursions. In 2005 we decided to sell the earthbag house and move to Mexico, using CanDo as our base.

This led to finding some property with a small cabin on it near Lake Chapala, Mexico, which we bought. CanDo then became our casita for overnight guests, and we lived in the cabin for five years.

Now we are back in the small community in Colorado in another house, and CanDo continues to be our casita and occasional excursion vehicle. Who knows where it will take us next?